The
BIBLE
MAP
for Kids

The BIBLE MAP for Kids

Tracy M. Sumner

A Surprisingly EASY GUIDE to God's Word

BARBOUR **kidz**
A Division of Barbour Publishing

Published by Barbour Publishing, Inc., 1810 Barbour Drive, Uhrichsville, Ohio 44683, www.barbourbooks.com

Our mission is to inspire the world with the life-changing message of the Bible.

ecpa Member of the
Evangelical Christian
Publishers Association

Printed in China.

001573 0523 DS

CONTENTS

Welcome to the
SEVEN "LANDS"
OF THE BIBLE

When you want to explore the Bible, you'll need a map. That's what this surprisingly easy guide to scripture is all about.

The Bible Map will walk you through seven different "lands" of God's Word:

- ▶ **Origins:** where everything comes from
- ▶ **Sin:** the problem that affects everyone
- ▶ **God's People:** Israel as a blessing to all nations
- ▶ **Exile:** the sin and decline of God's people
- ▶ **the Messiah:** Jesus' life and teaching, death and resurrection
- ▶ **Christianity:** the birth and growth of the church
- ▶ **the End Times:** Jesus' return and the renewal of all things

The "main road" of the Bible features highlights of God's Word in the order in which they happened. Short paragraphs explain what was happening in Bible times, always with an eye toward God's love for people. Meanwhile, "side roads" are also explored, to help you understand some of the strange and confusing parts of the Bible.

As you read *The Bible Map for Kids*, you'll learn more about the God who made you, who loves you, and who longs for you to be part of His family. Read on for a life-changing journey through scripture!

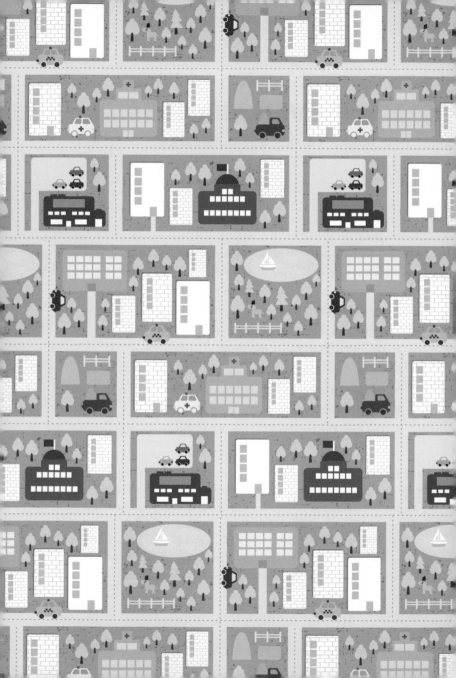

MAIN ROAD

God Creates the Universe and the Earth (Genesis 1:1–10, 14–19)

The book of Genesis, the very first book of the Bible, begins with the words, "In the beginning God created the heaven and the earth." But our world then looked a lot different than it does now!

Genesis 1:2 (NLV) says, "The earth was an empty waste and darkness was over the deep waters." Our world wasn't yet ready for humans—or any life at all. But over the next five days, God formed this world into a version that was perfect for human life.

God Creates Life (Genesis 1:11–13, 20–31)

On the first creation day (Genesis 1:1–5), God made the heavens and the earth, as well as light. He created the sky (our atmosphere) on day 2 (verses 6–8). On day 3 (verses 9–13), God formed dry land and made the first living things—plants. On day 4 (verses 14–19), He created the sun, moon, and stars. On day 5 (verses 20–23) God introduced birds and everything that swims. And on day 6 (verses 24–31) He created creatures that live on dry land. . .including people!

Where Did God Come From?

The Bible starts with the words "In the beginning God created. . ." This means everything He made had a beginning. But what about God? Where did He come from?

The Bible says nothing about God having any kind of beginning. In fact, Moses, the man who wrote the first books of the Bible, said, "Before the mountains were brought forth or You had ever formed the earth and the world, even from everlasting to everlasting, You are God" (Psalm 90:2).

In other words, God has just always been around. God's own name for Himself reflects this truth: "I Am That I Am" (Exodus 3:14).

It's hard to understand, isn't it? That's because God is far beyond our human understanding. That's just who He is!

God Creates Humanity (Genesis 1:26–30, 2:21–25)

On the first five days of creation, God showed His unlimited power and creativity. But when He came to the best part—human beings—He showed His love.

After five days of preparing, God used the simple dirt He'd already created to form the first man, called Adam. He made Adam to have a loving, personal relationship with Him—much like a kid relates to a loving parent.

Then, from Adam's own body, God created a partner for him—Eve. God blessed them both and said, "Give birth to many. Grow in number. Fill the earth and rule over it. Rule over the fish of the sea, over the birds of the sky, and over every living thing that moves on the earth" (Genesis 1:28 NLV).

In His Image (Genesis 1:26–27)

God created every living thing on the earth, but we humans are the only ones made in His own "image." This means we reflect God's nature in very important ways. For example, we have the ability to think and communicate like He does. We were also created to rule over the earth and all the animals.

The Bible says that God "breathed into [Adam's] nostrils the breath of life, and man became a living soul" (Genesis 2:7). At that point, Adam gained the ability to do something none of the animals could: connect with God in a personal, loving way.

Where Was the Garden of Eden?

"The Lord God planted a garden to the east in Eden. He put the man there whom He had made. And the Lord God made to grow out of the ground every tree that is pleasing to the eyes and good for food. And He made the tree of life grow in the center of the garden, and the tree of learning of good and bad" (Genesis 2:8–9 NLV).

The garden of Eden was likely a beautiful place filled with delicious food for Adam and Eve and their kids. Though the Bible never says where it was, it does say that "a river flowed out of Eden to water the garden. And from there it divided and became four rivers" (Genesis 2:10 NLV). Those four rivers were named Pishon, Gihon, Tigris, and Euphrates.

The Pishon and Gihon rivers have been lost to history, but the Tigris and Euphrates both flow to this day. If we assume those two rivers are the same ones that Genesis mentions, then the garden of Eden would have been somewhere in the Middle East, probably in modern-day Iraq.

God Creates Marriage (Genesis 2:18–24)

Before God created Eve, He had placed Adam in the garden of Eden and told him to take care of it (Genesis 2:15). But God knew something was missing: every creature in the garden had a partner. . .except for Adam.

God said to Himself, "It is not good that the man should be alone; I will make him a help suitable for him" (Genesis 2:18). So God put Adam into a deep sleep and then took a rib from his side. From this, God created Eve to be Adam's wife.

Adam loved what he saw when he first met Eve. "This is now bone of my bones and flesh of my flesh," he exclaimed. "She shall be called Woman, because she was taken out of Man" (Genesis 2:23). And with that, marriage was born! That's why when people get older, they leave their mom and dad to marry someone they love (see Genesis 2:24).

God Rests (Genesis 2:1–3)

Genesis 2 is mostly about God's creation of human beings, but the first three verses review the entire creation week. Verse 2 says, "God ended His work that He had made, and He rested on the seventh day from all His work that He had made."

Why did God "rest"? Because He got tired? No. He rested as an example for *us*—so we can set apart one day of rest from each seven-day week (verse 3). Many years later, God made that day of rest a law for His chosen people, the Israelites (Exodus 20:8–11).

How Does Genesis 2 Match Up with Genesis 1?

Genesis 1 and Genesis 2 tell different versions of the same creation story. Genesis 1 describes all six creation days, while Genesis 2 focuses on the sixth day—when people were made.

Some people who don't believe the Bible say Genesis 1 and Genesis 2 contradict each other—they don't match up. Genesis 1:11, they say, describes God creating plants on the third day, but Genesis 2:5 says this happened after He made humans, on the sixth day. The solution is pretty simple: Genesis 1:11 talks about plant life in general, but Genesis 2:5 describes the plants Adam could care for and harvest for food.

Another example: Genesis 1:24–25 says God created the animals early on the sixth creation day, but Genesis 2:19–20 seems to say that God created the animals *after* He created Adam. But once again, there's no problem here. The second account just says God had already created the animals and then brought them to Adam "to see what he would call them" (Genesis 2:19). That's when Adam gave all the animals their names. (Bet that took awhile!)

MAIN ROAD

A Choice to Make (Genesis 2:15–17)

Adam and Eve had it made. They were in charge of a beautiful garden, which their Creator visited every day. They could eat (almost) any plant that grew there. There was no sin or death—in fact, they didn't even know what those were! Adam and Eve were set to live like this forever.

God had given the couple just one rule to follow: "You are free to eat from any tree of the garden. But do not eat from the tree of learning of good and bad. For the day you eat from it you will die for sure" (Genesis 2:16–17 NLV).

Sadly, Adam and Eve chose to disobey.

The Saddest Day in History (Genesis 3)

The first humans had nothing to fear—they lived in peace with God and with all the animals in the garden. But one day as Eve was by herself in the garden, a talking serpent slithered up to her. (The Bible's final book, Revelation, identifies this "old serpent" as Satan, the devil.)

The snake then pointed her to the tree whose fruit God had told them not to eat. "You shall not surely die," he lied, "for God knows that in the day you eat from it, then your eyes shall be opened and you shall be as gods, knowing good and evil" (Genesis 3:4–5).

Eve took the bait. She picked a fruit and took a bite. . .then handed some to Adam. Surely, Adam would know better, right? Wrong. He took the fruit from Eve's hand and ate it too.

What Is "Original Sin"?

Because Adam and Eve disobeyed God, they suffered. And their kids, their kids' kids, and everyone down through history would be born into sin.

This is known as "original sin"—and it's the worst thing to ever happen to humanity. Sin ruins us and separates us from God. That's why Adam and Eve hid from Him after they disobeyed (Genesis 3:6).

Here are some verses that tell how original sin affects every one of us:

▶ "[People] have all turned aside. Together they have become bad. There is no one who does good, not even one" (Psalm 14:3 NLV).

▶ "Sin came into the world by one man, Adam. Sin brought death with it. Death spread to all men because all have sinned" (Romans 5:12 NLV).

▶ "Adam did not obey God, and many people become sinners through him. Christ obeyed God and makes many people right with Himself" (Romans 5:19 NLV).

▶ "Death came because of a man, Adam. Being raised from the dead also came because of a Man, Christ. All men will die as Adam died. But all those who belong to Christ will be raised to new life" (1 Corinthians 15:21–22 NLV).

How Sin Changed Everything (Genesis 3:6–13)

The moment Adam and Eve ate the forbidden fruit, everything changed. For one thing, they both felt guilt for the first time. And they were embarrassed for walking around the garden naked, so they used fig leaves to hide their bodies.

Worst of all, Adam and Eve became *afraid* of God for the first time—so afraid that they hid themselves from Him (see Genesis 3:10).

Sin Brought Death (Genesis 3:14–24)

It was a terrible day for Adam and Eve, and for every person who would live after them. Though God had said they would die if they ate from the tree of the knowledge of good and evil, this didn't happen immediately. . .not physically, at least. When Adam and Eve chose to sin, they died *spiritually*. Now, their relationship with the God who had created them and who loved them was ruined.

This is why the New Testament says that "the wages of sin is death" (Romans 6:23).

God's Plan to Fix the Sin Problem

Bad news: the whole world was now under a curse because of Adam and Eve's sin. Good news: God had a plan to fix things!

That plan was to one day send a Messiah—a Savior—into the world to rescue people from sin. On the same day He sent Adam and Eve out of the garden of Eden, He made the first prophecy about the Messiah: "I will make you [the serpent] and the woman hate each other, and your seed and her seed will hate each other. He will crush your head, and you will crush his heel" (Genesis 3:15 NLV).

While this verse doesn't use the words *Jesus* or *Savior*, the idea is certainly there. He would be the descendant—the family member—of Eve who would defeat the devil once and for all!

Though Adam and Eve failed in the worst possible way, they were still God's most prized creation. God would not simply hand them—nor any of their descendants—over to the devil.

God's Curses for Sin (Genesis 3:14–24)

Adam and Eve's sin stained humanity and all of nature. Every good thing—even the act of growing crops—would now come with hard work. The relationship between husbands and wives would be strained. Babies would be born with pain. Everyone would eventually die.

God made Adam and Eve leave the garden and placed a cherub (a type of angel) to guard the entrance so they couldn't return.

Sin Takes Hold of Humanity (Genesis 4, 6–10)

Genesis 4 tells about the first murder. In a fit of jealousy, Cain—the world's first child—killed his younger brother because God had accepted Abel's sacrifice but not Cain's.

From this time forward, humans became more and more evil. Things got so bad that God destroyed the whole world—and every living thing on it—with a huge flood. God told the world's only good man, Noah, to build a giant boat called an "ark." It would save him, his family, and two of every kind of animal from the floodwaters.

After that, human beings would once again fill the world.

Did God Flood the Whole World?

Some people believe that God flooded just the parts of the world where people lived. But the Bible clearly teaches that the entire earth was covered: "All the high hills that were under the whole heaven were covered" (Genesis 7:19), and "all flesh died that moved on the earth, both of fowl, and of cattle, and of beast, and of every creeping thing that creeps on the earth, and every man" (verse 21). Only Noah, his family, and the animals on the ark stayed alive.

In addition to what the Bible says, there is scientific evidence of a worldwide flood. Every continent in the world contains tons of fossils, remains of things that lived long ago. And huge deposits of coal and oil show that lots of plants were rapidly covered by water and mud.

3. GOD'S PEOPLE
Israel as a Blessing to All Nations

MAIN ROAD

God Builds a Great Nation (Genesis 12–50)

In Genesis 3:14–15, God hinted that a Messiah would save human beings from the consequences of their sin. God didn't send Jesus into the world immediately, "but at the right time, God sent His Son. A woman gave birth to Him under the Law. This all happened so He could buy with His blood and make free all those who were held by the Law. Then we might become the sons of God" (Galatians 4:4–5 NLV).

Starting in Genesis 12, the Bible shifts gears, telling how God began to set up the nation of Israel. That's where the Messiah would come from one day.

Israel's Founding Fathers (Genesis 12–50)

Israel's earliest leaders are called patriarchs. (The word *patriarch* means "father.")

In Genesis, these patriarchs were Abraham (Genesis 11:26–25:8), Isaac (21:1–35:28), and Jacob, whom God renamed "Israel" (25:21–50:14). These men were the fathers of the nation of Israel.

Jacob had twelve sons, and together, these families grew into the "twelve tribes of Israel." These tribes were sometimes known as Jews, Hebrews, or Israelites. In time, they would become a fully formed nation with kings like Saul, David, and Solomon.

The Importance of the Nation of Israel

The nation of Israel played a huge role in the Bible. . .and in God's plan to save the world.

In Genesis 12:1–3, God provided more detail about this plan: the Messiah would be a descendant of Abraham, Isaac, and Jacob—Israel's patriarchs.

Long before Jesus' birth, God wanted Israel to be an example of what serving Him really looks like. Israel was to teach other nations about the Lord. Sadly, Israel usually failed in that assignment—but God still loved His people.

Hundreds of years after the patriarchs, God said through the prophet Isaiah, "But now listen. . .Israel whom I have chosen. This is what the Lord Who made you. . .says, 'Do not be afraid, O Jacob My servant' " (Isaiah 44:1–2 NLV).

This—and many other scriptures—make it clear just how special Israel was to God.

God Calls Abraham (Genesis 12)

God chose Abraham (originally called Abram) to be father of the nation of Israel—as well as the spiritual father to Jews and Christians alike. Because of that, he's one of the most important people in the Bible.

This is what God said to Abram:

> *"Leave your country. . .and go to the land that I will show you. And I will make you a great nation. . . . I will make your name great, so you will be honored. I will bring good to those who are good to you. And I will curse those who curse you. Good will come to all the families of the earth because of you."*
>
> GENESIS 12:1–3 NLV

God's Promise to Abram (Genesis 15)

Abram didn't question God. . .or even ask where he and his family were going! He simply obeyed, leaving Haran and journeying to Canaan, some six hundred miles away.

Many years passed and Abram became old, still having no children of his own. Suddenly, God appeared to him and made an amazing covenant, or promise: "Look now toward heaven and count the stars, if you are able to number them. . . . So shall your descendants be" (Genesis 15:5). God was very pleased that Abram believed (Genesis 15:6).

God was about to do a great miracle in the lives of Abram and his wife, Sarai. Like Abram, she would also get a name change: Sarah.

Why Did God Choose Abram?

Genesis doesn't explain why God chose Abram to be the father of the Hebrew nation. The New Testament, however, hints that God chose him because of his faith:

> *Because Abraham had faith, he obeyed God when God called him to leave his home. . . . His faith in God kept him living as a stranger in the country God had promised to him. . . . Abraham was looking to God and waiting for a city that could not be moved. It was a city planned and built by God.*
> HEBREWS 11:8–10 NLV

Like everyone else, Abraham was not perfect. But he believed God, and that made God happy. The Bible shows Abraham as an example of what it takes to please God—believing Him enough to obey His commands.

God's Promise of a Miracle Baby (Genesis 17)

To fulfill His promise to make Abraham the father of a great nation, God made *another* promise to Abraham and his wife: "I will bless [Sarah] and give you a son from her also. . . . She shall be a mother of nations. Kings of people shall be from her" (Genesis 17:16).

At first, Abraham just laughed (Genesis 17:17). He was a hundred years old! Sarah was ninety. How could they have a child? But God told Abraham, "Sarah will give birth to your son. And you will give him the name Isaac. I will make My agreement with him and for his children after him, an agreement that will last forever. . . . [Isaac] will be born to Sarah at this time next year" (verses 19, 21 NLV).

God Lives Up to His Promise (Genesis 18, 21)

When Sarah heard God's promise to give her a son, she laughed inside. *I'm much too old to have a baby*, she thought. But God knew that she'd laughed, and He asked Abraham, "For what reason did Sarah laugh. . . ? Is anything too hard for the LORD?" (Genesis 18:13–14).

God always keeps His promises. He sent a miracle baby to the old couple, Abraham and Sarah. Sarah was amazed (Genesis 21:7).

God would use Isaac in building the nation of Israel. That was how God planned to bring salvation to the world.

Why Did God Tell Abraham to Kill Isaac?

One day, God told Abraham to do something really hard: "Take now your son, your only son Isaac, whom you love, and get into the land of Moriah, and offer him there for a burnt offering on one of the mountains of which I will tell you" (Genesis 22:2). What Abraham didn't know was that God was testing his faith.

Abraham obeyed, taking Isaac to Moriah and building an altar. But at the last second, the Lord's angel stepped in and stopped him. God said to Abraham:

> *"Because you have done this and have not kept from Me your son, your only son. . .I will add many to the number of your children and all who come after them, like the stars of the heavens and the sand beside the sea. They will take over the cities of those who hate them. Good will come to all the nations of the earth by your children and their children's children. Because you have obeyed My voice."*
>
> GENESIS 22:16–18 NLV

What a great example of obedience! Even when God's command didn't make sense to him, Abraham trusted God to keep His promises. At the last minute, God came through for everyone.

God Continues the Family Line (Genesis 24–25)

Isaac was forty years old when he married a woman named Rebekah. She was not able to have a child, at least without God's help. So Isaac prayed, and God blessed Rebekah with twins: Jacob and Esau.

God then told Rebekah that these twins were "two nations." One would be stronger than the other, "and the elder shall serve the younger" (Genesis 25:23). Though Jacob was born after Esau, he would eventually join the line of the patriarchs of Israel.

Jacob Steals His Brother's Birthright (Genesis 25:24–34)

The name *Jacob* means "deceiver". . .and he certainly lived up (or down) to his name. Jacob had his strengths, but he was also dishonest and willing to do almost anything to get what he wanted.

Esau had been born first, so he was entitled to his father's wealth after Isaac died. But Jacob, wanting the riches for himself, tricked his brother into selling his birthright. . .for a single bowl of soup. Later, Jacob and his mother, Rebekah, managed to trick Isaac into giving Jacob his fatherly blessing!

As a result, the Jewish people descended from Jacob—not Esau (see Genesis 27).

How Could God Use a Man Like Jacob?

You probably wouldn't want to meet someone like Jacob. He was a cheat and a liar who did really wrong things to his brother and father. But God didn't bless Jacob because he deserved goodness—God blessed Jacob as part of His plan to bless the whole world through Israel.

One time, afraid that Esau was coming to get him, Jacob prayed to God, "I am not worthy of the least of all the mercies. . .which You have shown to Your servant. . . . Deliver me, I ask You, from the hand of my brother" (Genesis 32:10–11). Then he reminded God of His promises and asked Him to keep His word.

God continued to work, making Jacob a patriarch to His chosen people. God also renamed Jacob "Israel," which means "one who has struggled with God" (Genesis 32:22–31). Later, God's chosen nation was named after him.

Jacob's Twelve Sons (Genesis 35, 37)

Jacob fathered twelve sons. Each of them fathered families that came to be known as the "twelve tribes of Israel."

But Jacob's family had problems. The Bible says that "Israel [Jacob] loved Joseph more than all his children. . .and he made him a coat of many colors. And. . .his brothers. . .hated him and could not speak peaceably to him" (Genesis 37:3–4).

Joseph made matters worse by tattling to Jacob whenever his brothers did bad things. Finally, when Joseph told his brothers he'd dreamed that they all bowed down to him (Genesis 37:5–11), they became angry enough to take action.

How God Brought Joseph to Egypt (Genesis 37:12–36)

Because Joseph's father favored him—and because Joseph angered his older brothers with his own words—the ten older sons started plotting murder.

But the firstborn, Reuben, put a stop to his brothers' plan. He said, "Do not shed blood, but cast him into this pit that is in the wilderness, and lay no hand on him" (Genesis 37:22).

Reuben planned to return later and rescue Joseph. But while Reuben was away, the other brothers pulled Joseph out of the dry well and sold him! Joseph went with a group of Ishmaelites who were carrying items to sell in Egypt. They took him to Egypt, where Joseph became a slave.

Why Do Bad Things Happen to Good People?

Hated by his brothers, thrown into a dry well, and sold as a slave, Joseph found even more trouble in Egypt. He was sent to prison after his master's wife lied, accusing him of something terrible. Still, Joseph held to what was right in God's eyes. He set an example for all of us today.

God never promised that His people wouldn't suffer. Instead, He sometimes allows hard things when He knows they will help His plans come to reality.

That is why Joseph could tell his brothers, "You planned to do a bad thing to me. But God planned it for good, to make it happen that many people should be kept alive, as they are today" (Genesis 50:20 NLV).

Joseph's Life in Egypt (Genesis 39–41)

Even though Joseph was a slave in Egypt, his master really liked him—and soon gave him a big promotion. Unfortunately, the master's wife fell in love with Joseph. He knew God wanted him to say no to her, and he tried to avoid her. She got mad and lied that Joseph had committed a crime. He was thrown in prison.

While there, Joseph interpreted dreams for two other prisoners, who were servants of Pharaoh, the king of Egypt. This came in handy when Pharaoh himself had a dream and needed someone to explain it!

Joseph told Pharaoh that his dream warned of a coming famine. And Joseph gave the king advice for dealing with the disaster.

Pharaoh was so impressed that he put Joseph in charge of the entire land of Egypt.

The Hebrews Travel to Egypt (Genesis 42–50)

When the time of famine came, Egypt had more than enough grain stored away thanks to Joseph's wise advice.

Back in Canaan (later to be called Israel), the famine was causing fear. When Jacob heard there was plenty of food in Egypt, he sent his sons to buy what they could. They didn't realize the important man who sold the food was their brother Joseph! They bowed to him, just as the young man had dreamed many years before.

Joseph forgave his brothers. And Jacob, who thought for years that Joseph was dead, was finally able to see his beloved son again.

Jacob's family of seventy people then moved to Egypt, where Joseph took care of them.

The Book of Job

Many Bible experts believe Job lived around the time of the patriarchs. At the beginning of the book, this godly man was very wealthy, with thousands of animals. He also had ten kids and many servants (Job 1:2–3).

As the story begins, the devil tells God that Job only served Him for the blessings he'd receive (Job 1:8–11). God knew that wasn't true. So He allowed the devil to test Job's faith with a series of terrible attacks. Job lost all of his wealth, his kids, and his own health.

Even worse, four of his "friends" accused him of sinning in secret. Why else, they asked, would all of these bad things be happening?

In the end, Job spoke face-to-face with God and realized that He knew best. Job knew his Lord more deeply, and he was blessed with another family and twice his original wealth.

Making a Home in Egypt (Exodus 1)

The Israelites stayed in Egypt, in a region called Goshen, for about 430 years after Jacob and his family arrived from Canaan. During that time, they built homes, married, and had lots of children. But many years later, a new pharaoh grew worried. He was afraid the Israelites would become too powerful to control. So he made God's people slaves. He even called for all the Hebrew boys to be killed at birth!

God Sees His People's Afflictions. . . and Acts (Exodus 2–3)

God saw how much His people were suffering in Egypt. So when the time was right, He told a man named Moses to lead the people out of their slavery.

As an Israelite, Moses had miraculously escaped Pharaoh's command to drown male babies in the Nile River. Amazingly, he was adopted by Pharaoh's daughter! But Moses never forgot his Israelite beginnings.

One day, Moses killed an Egyptian slave driver who was abusing a Hebrew. Then he ran away to a place called Midian. There, God spoke to Moses from a burning bush: "I have seen the suffering of My people in Egypt. I have heard their cry because of the men who make them work. I know how they suffer," God told him. "Now come, and I will send you to Pharaoh so that you may bring My people, the sons of Israel, out of Egypt" (Exodus 3:7, 10 NLV).

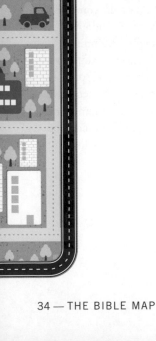

SIDE ROAD

What Makes Moses So Important?

Moses was a great deliverer who freed his fellow Israelites from Egyptian slavery.

He stood up to Pharaoh. He stuck to God's commands when Pharaoh mocked the Lord. He led God's people through the Red Sea, which was split in two by the power of God. He wandered with the people for years in the wilderness. He received the laws God wanted His people to follow (including the Ten Commandments). And he wrote the first five books of the Bible (Genesis, Exodus, Leviticus, Numbers, and Deuteronomy, known together as the "Pentateuch").

The most impressive thing about Moses is this: he was called a friend of God (Exodus 33:11).

Moses: Not Eager to Lead (Exodus 4)

Moses was a hero to both Jews and Christians because of his leadership of God's people.

But Moses didn't obey God right away. In fact, he told God that he wasn't good enough. Moses complained that he wasn't a great speaker. His excuses angered God. But the Lord still promised to be with Moses as he went to Egypt to tell Pharaoh what to do. And God gave Moses miraculous powers to use while facing the Egyptian ruler.

Finally, God told Moses' brother, Aaron, to speak for Moses: "I know that he can speak well," God said. "You shall speak to him and put words in his mouth" (Exodus 4:14–15).

Moses Confronts Pharaoh (Exodus 5)

When Moses demanded that Pharaoh let God's people go, the Egyptian king refused. "I do not know the LORD," he said, "neither will I let Israel go" (Exodus 5:2).

But Pharaoh didn't get the last word. To break his stubbornness, God sent ten terrible plagues on Egypt—the Nile River turning to blood (Exodus 7:17–18), frogs (8:1–4), lice (8:16–17), flies (8:20–22), the death of livestock (9:1–4), sores (9:8–9), hail (9:22–23), locusts (10:4–5), darkness (10:21–22), and the death of all firstborn (11:4–7).

Passover

Passover celebrates the Israelites' departure (or "exodus") from Egypt. It is still an important Jewish holiday. When God said He was going to wipe out all the firstborn of humans and livestock in Egypt, He told the Israelites to smear lamb's blood over the doors of their homes. God would "pass over" every home that had the blood. After this plague, Pharaoh finally ordered the Israelites to leave Egypt (Exodus 12:31–32).

Blood is an important thing in the Bible. When people in Old Testament times sinned, they had to shed the blood of a flawless animal as a "sacrifice." This meant that the person did not have to die for his own sin—the sin was covered, at least for a while, by the sacrifice. Much later, Jesus became the flawless, once-for-all sacrifice for all humanity. When the blood of the perfect "Passover Lamb" was shed, all other sacrifices came to an end. Now, faith in Jesus' work removes our sin.

The Israelites Leave Egypt (Exodus 12)

After the death of all the firstborn in Egypt—including his own son—Pharaoh finally let the Israelites go. That night, he told Moses and Aaron, "Get up and go away from my people, both you and the people of Israel. Go and worship the Lord, as you have said" (Exodus 12:31 NLV).

The people of Israel—about six hundred thousand men plus many more women and children—left Egypt, carrying a lot of Egypt's best things with them (Exodus 12:36).

Pharaoh's Last Shot (Exodus 14)

The Bible says that after the Hebrews left Egypt, "the LORD hardened the heart of Pharaoh, king of Egypt, and he pursued after the children of Israel" (Exodus 14:8). But God miraculously parted the Red Sea for them and led the people through. Then He drowned Pharaoh's army by crashing the waters back down!

The Israelites were now free to journey to the promised land. Along the way, they would see many more miracles, suffer a lot of God's correction, and receive laws that would control their lives in Canaan.

The Promised Land

God freed the Israelites from their Egyptian slavery so that they could make the journey to the promised land.

This land was also called Canaan, named after a grandson of Noah. It lay mostly between the Mediterranean Sea and the Jordan River. God had promised this land to Abraham and his descendants in Genesis 12:7. He guided the people of Israel to their promised land by His own presence and through His miracle power. In Canaan, they would build up their nation called Israel (Exodus 33:14–16).

God Gives Moses the Ten Commandments
(Exodus 19–20)

The Israelites had seen God perform awesome miracles to break them out of Egypt and provide for them.

Three months after they left Egypt, the Israelites camped in the wilderness at the bottom of Mount Sinai. Moses climbed the mountain, where he spent forty days alone with God. The Lord wrote the Ten Commandments on two stone tablets. Then He gave them to Moses and told him to carry them back down the mountain.

The Purpose of the Ten Commandments
(Exodus 20:1–17)

God also gave Moses hundreds of other rules for the people. The Ten Commandments are a quick summary of all those rules. They were designed to guide God's people in their new lives in the promised land.

The first of God's Ten Commandments says, "You shall have no other gods before Me" (Exodus 20:3). God had chosen the people of Israel as His own. He brought them out of slavery in Egypt. He established them as a nation. God had no desire to share their love with some false god.

The Ten Commandments

▶ You shall have no other gods before Me.

▶ You shall not make for yourself any graven image, or any likeness of anything that is in heaven above, or that is in the earth beneath, or that is in the water under the earth.

▶ You shall not take the name of the LORD your God in vain, for the LORD will not hold him guiltless who takes His name in vain.

▶ Remember the Sabbath day, to keep it holy. Six days you shall labor and do all your work, but the seventh day is the Sabbath of the LORD your God.

▶ Honor your father and your mother, that your days may be long on the land that the LORD your God gives you.

▶ You shall not kill.

▶ You shall not commit adultery.

▶ You shall not steal.

▶ You shall not bear false witness against your neighbor.

▶ You shall not covet your neighbor's house. You shall not covet your neighbor's wife, or his manservant, or his maidservant, or his ox, or his donkey, or anything that is your neighbor's.

God Gives the Israelites the Law (Leviticus)

God delivered the Israelites out of Egypt. Then, through Moses, God told the people how to live, how to treat one another, and how to worship. These laws are found in the book of Leviticus. The book also describes the way to sacrifice when the laws were broken.

According to ancient Jewish tradition, the law of Moses contains 613 commandments. Each law fits into one of three categories: civil, ceremonial, or moral.

Types of Laws (Leviticus)

Civil laws were the rules of daily living. They dealt with things such as kindness for the poor (Leviticus 19:9–10), debt (Leviticus 25:35–46), theft (Leviticus 19:11), and many other topics.

Ceremonial laws involved Israel's worship of God. They included festivals (Leviticus 23), rules for food (Leviticus 11), the duties of priests (Leviticus 8–9), and various sin offerings (Leviticus 1–7).

Finally, moral laws concerned the way people should live to reflect God's holy nature. They include laws concerning idolatry (Leviticus 19:4) and how to treat your parents (Leviticus 19:3). These laws are still in effect for Christians today.

Why Do Christians Follow Some Laws of Leviticus but Not Others?

God expects Christians today to follow His moral laws, which are all repeated in the New Testament. The civil laws, however, were just for the ancient nation of Israel. The ceremonial laws were all fulfilled when Jesus sacrificed Himself on the cross.

Jesus' own teachings (and the rest of the New Testament) tell us that God does not require Christians to follow Old Testament laws on food, animal sacrifices, feasts, and so on (see Romans 2:25–29, Galatians 2:15–16, and Ephesians 2:15, for example). The New Testament, which came into effect with Jesus' life, death, and resurrection, is our guide now. It is God's most up-to-date message to His people.

God Leads His People toward the Promised Land (Numbers)

The book of Numbers tells of the Israelites' journey from Mount Sinai to the border of Canaan, the beautiful promised land God had already given them. But the people's unbelief, complaining, and disobedience led to a punishment of *forty years* of wandering in the wilderness.

God Delays the Israelites' Entry into the Promised Land (Numbers 13–14)

Moses sent twelve spies—one from each tribe—to scout out the promised land. Ten of the spies returned with frightening reports of giants in the land. But the other two spies, Joshua and Caleb, believed the Israelites could easily take the land. Why? Because God was with them.

Sadly, the Israelites listened to the negative report.

God was so angry that He was ready to destroy the Israelites and make a new nation from Moses' family. But Moses prayed for the people, and God spared them. However, God said that Israel would not enter the promised land for another forty years. Joshua and Caleb, the two good spies, would live to see Canaan.

The "Good Spies" of Israel

When twelve spies were sent ahead to spy out the promised land, only Joshua and Caleb gave a positive report.

Joshua is first mentioned in the Bible in Exodus 17:9. Moses commanded him to choose and lead men in battle against the Amalekites, who lived south of Canaan. Later, Joshua would heroically lead the Israelites into their promised land.

Caleb was very bold. He asked for a section of the promised land when he was eighty-five, promising to drive out any giants he found there (Joshua 14:6–15)!

Joshua and Caleb were faithful men who believed God's promises and acted on them. They recognized the strength of the giants of Canaan. But they knew their God was far more powerful.

Moses Makes a Big Mistake (Numbers 20:7–12)

Moses had led the people of Israel brilliantly, but God didn't let him enter the promised land.

When the people were complaining of thirst, God told Moses to speak to a large rock. It would then miraculously put out water. Moses was angry with the people's grumbling, though, and he hit the rock with his shepherd's staff instead.

God still provided the water. But He told Moses, "Because you have not believed Me and honored Me as holy in the eyes of the people of Israel, you will not bring these people into the land I have given them" (Numbers 20:12 NLV).

The Miracle of the Bronze Serpent (Numbers 21:5–9)

The Israelites' complained a lot. In response, God sent poisonous snakes into their camp.

As people suffered and died, Moses prayed for them. God told him to form a snake out of a metal called bronze. Anyone who'd been bitten by a real snake could look at the bronze serpent and be healed.

Many centuries later, Jesus compared Himself to that bronze serpent. He said, "As Moses lifted up the serpent in the wilderness, even so the Son of Man must be lifted up, that whoever believes in Him should not perish but have eternal life" (John 3:14–15).

The Sad, Strange Story of Balaam

Moab was a nation that often fought against Israel. Balak, the king of Moab, wanted a man named Balaam to curse Israel. But God warned Balaam to speak only the Lord's words.

When Balaam saddled his donkey to go meet Balak, God stopped Balaam by sending an angel to block the animal's path. Balaam beat the poor donkey three times. . .before God gave it the ability to talk (Numbers 22:28). Balaam noticed the angel just in time—the angel was about to kill him!

In Moab, Balak ordered Balaam three times to curse Israel. But each time, Balaam spoke a blessing instead. The king was really angry, and he sent the prophet away without pay.

The "Second Law" (Deuteronomy)

Deuteronomy is the fifth and final book of the Pentateuch. In it, Moses spoke to the Israelites who were born after God had delivered their parents and grandparents from Egypt.

Many of the younger Israelites had probably heard about what God had done for the older people. But now that they were about to enter the promised land, Moses wanted to remind them of God's law. (*Deuteronomy* means "second law.")

Moses spoke to the people four times. He reminded them where they'd come from, who they belonged to, and how they should live.

Moses' Death (Deuteronomy 34)

Moses had been an excellent leader for Israel over the last forty years of his life. Sadly, though, a choice to disobey God prevented him from leading the people into the promised land.

The last chapter of Deuteronomy says Moses climbed to the top of Mount Nebo, where God showed him the promised land of Canaan (Deuteronomy 34:4).

Moses then died, outside the promised land, at the age of 120. Then God "buried him in a valley in the land of Moab, across from Beth-peor, but no man knows of his burial place to this day" (verse 6).

Joshua

Under Moses' leadership, Joshua had led soldiers into battle against Amalek (Exodus 17:9) and scouted out the promised land (Numbers 13).

But now God told Moses, "See, the time for you to die is near. Call Joshua, and go to the meeting tent, so I may tell him what to do" (Deuteronomy 31:14 NLV). Moses and Joshua did as God commanded, and Joshua took charge.

Deuteronomy 34:9 says, "Joshua the son of Nun was full of the spirit of wisdom, for Moses had laid his hands on him. And the children of Israel listened to him and did as the LORD commanded Moses."

New Leader, Same Mission (Joshua 1)

After the death of Moses, Joshua took charge.

God had given Joshua a job that was impossible to do in his own strength—capturing and settling the promised land! But God told him, "Be strong and of good courage. Do not be afraid or be dismayed, for the LORD your God is with you wherever you go" (Joshua 1:9). Joshua believed God and got to work.

Because of that, God made Joshua a great leader in the eyes of all his people (Joshua 4:14).

Israel's Miraculous Entry into Canaan (Joshua 3–4)

To enter the promised land, the Israelites had to cross the Jordan River. But there were no bridges or boats—and the river was overflowing its banks! God, however, can always make a way. He stopped up the river far upstream, allowing the Israelites to cross on the dry riverbed (Joshua 3:15–17).

After hundreds of years of waiting, the Israelites were now in the land God had promised them.

The Memorial of the Twelve Stones

After all the Israelites had crossed the Jordan River, God commanded Joshua, "Choose twelve men from the people, one man from each family. Tell them, 'Take twelve stones from the middle of the Jordan. Take them from the place where the religious leaders' feet are standing. Carry them over with you, and lay them down in the place where you stay tonight'" (Joshua 4:2–3 NLV).

Joshua then told the stone carriers that these rocks would serve as "a memorial to the children of Israel forever" (Joshua 4:7).

The men placed the stones in the middle of the riverbed where the priests had stood. The Bible says, "They are there to this day" (Joshua 4:9).

The Israelites' Work in Canaan (Joshua 6–21)

The book of Joshua tells how Israel took over the promised land of Canaan. They defeated the super-strong city of Jericho (chapter 6), the city of Ai (chapter 7), all of southern Canaan (chapters 9–10), and finally, a group of northern Canaanite kings (chapter 11).

Though the people of Israel had traveled as a group since leaving Egypt, they were still a collection of twelve tribes. Joshua's final task was to give each tribe its own section of the promised land. That story is told in Joshua 13–21.

Joshua's Goodbye (Joshua 24)

Shortly before Joshua died, he reminded the people of all the miracles God had done for them. And he encouraged the people to remain faithful to Him: "So fear the Lord. Serve Him in faith and truth. . . . If you think it is wrong to serve the Lord, choose today whom you will serve. . . . But as for me and my family, we will serve the Lord" (Joshua 24:14–15 NLV).

Joshua died at the age of 110. He was buried in a place called Timnath-serah.

The "Battle of Jericho"

Jericho was surrounded by high, thick walls that protected the city from even the most dangerous invaders. But God gave Joshua a strange battle plan for taking the city (Joshua 6:1–5).

Joshua would command his soldiers to march around the city once a day for six days. On the seventh day, the soldiers would march around the city seven times as the priests blew their horns. When the priests gave one long blast, all the people would shout. . .and the city would be theirs.

The "battle of Jericho" really wasn't much of a battle. The Israelites followed God's plan, and the walls came tumbling down (Joshua 6:20)!

Special Deliverers (Judges)

The book of Judges describes leaders called *"judges"*—but not the kind who sit in courtrooms. The word means "deliverer." These men (and one woman) bravely stepped up when the people of Israel, because they had disobeyed God, got into trouble with other nations. The judges were Othniel, Ehud, Shamgar, Deborah, Gideon, Abimelech, Tola, Jair, Jephthah, Ibzan, Elon, Abdon, and Samson.

The book of Judges describes a sad pattern: The people would follow God for a while and fall away. Next, God would allow other nations to trouble the Israelites until they cried out to Him. Then He would send a judge to deliver them from their enemies.

Othniel: Israel's First Judge (Judges 3:9–11)

Judges 3:7–8 (NLV) says that "the people of Israel did what was sinful in the eyes of the Lord. They forgot the Lord their God and served the Baals and the Asheroth [false gods]. So the anger of the Lord was against Israel. He sold them into the hand of Cushan-rishathaim king of Mesopotamia." Eight years later, the people of Israel cried out to God, who sent Othniel, Israel's first judge. Othniel rescued the Israelites, and they lived in peace for forty years.

How Could God Use a Man Like Samson?

Samson was the last judge in this book of the Bible (Judges 13–16). He showed great courage and strength fighting for Israel. The Bible says he once killed thirty enemy Philistines all by himself (Judges 14:19). Then he killed *a thousand* Philistines with the jawbone of a donkey (15:12–15). And he destroyed even more of his enemies by pushing down the pillars that held up their temple (16:26–30). Samson was able to do such things when "the Spirit of the LORD came mightily on him" (Judges 14:6).

Yet Samson wasn't the kind of man most of us would think a servant of God. He was selfish and prideful, always trying to get his own way. But Samson was still God's choice to judge Israel.

Judges 2:18 says, "When the LORD raised up judges for them, then the LORD was with the judge"—even one as messed up as Samson.

Judge Deborah (Judges 4:4–5:31)

Deborah was the fourth of the judges—and the only woman in the group. She became judge after Jabin, the king of Canaan, had ruled over Israel for twenty years. Deborah was also a prophetess, a wise and respected woman who spoke the words God gave her. Then, as a judge, she fought in the place of her military commander when he became afraid.

Because of her heroic leadership, Deborah is considered one of the most important women of the Bible.

Gideon, Israel's Greatest Judge (Judges 6:1–8:32)

God used Gideon—who was possibly Israel's greatest judge—to free Israel from the Midianites. His work led to peace in Israel for forty years.

With Gideon in the lead (but God truly in charge), three hundred Israelite warriors defeated a huge Midianite army. The Israelites wanted him to become their king, but Gideon was wise enough to say no. He knew God was the only King they needed (Judges 8:23).

Gideon lived to old age and was buried in his father's grave. Sadly, the people forgot God's deliverance and started worshipping a false god called Baal-berith.

Who Was Ruth. . .and Why Does She Matter?

Ruth was a young woman from Moab. She married into an Israelite family that had moved to Moab to escape a famine in Judah. Then Ruth's husband and father-in-law both died. She could have gone back to her own family in Moab, but Ruth promised to move with her mother-in-law, Naomi, to Bethlehem after the famine ended. There, Ruth met and married a wealthy farmer named Boaz.

Ruth played an important role in God's big plan of salvation. Though she was not an Israelite, she and Boaz had a son named Obed, who had a son named Jesse, who had a son named David—who became Israel's greatest king.

And eventually, David's family line led to Jesus Christ!

Prophets and Kings (1 Samuel)

The book of 1 Samuel tells two major stories. The first describes the beloved prophet Samuel, Israel's last judge (chapters 1–12). The rest of the book tells how the people began crying out for a king. . .and how God gave them what they wanted.

Saul, Israel's first king, didn't turn out so well. But God then chose a young shepherd named David to take the throne.

How Saul Became King (1 Samuel 8–10)

The prophet Samuel had two sons—Joel and Abijah—and he appointed both to be leaders. But Joel and Abijah were ungodly, selfish men. . .so the elders of Israel didn't trust them. They demanded a king to rule over Israel (1 Samuel 8:1–5).

God knew the people were really rejecting His own leadership. But He gave them a king anyway. God chose Saul, a tall, good-looking man who started his reign well. Saul got the Israelites to work together to defeat the enemy Philistines.

But pride led Saul to make some terrible decisions. After forty years, God removed him from the throne.

The Philistines

The Philistines pop up all throughout the Old Testament. These people lived southwest of Israel, between the Mediterranean Sea and the Jordan River. They worshipped false gods, loved to fight, and troubled Israel for several centuries. They even stole the ark of the covenant once, though that didn't turn out well for them (see 1 Samuel 4–5).

Early in Israel's history, God had promised to give the Philistines' land to His people (Exodus 23:31). But the Israelites didn't destroy everyone who lived in Canaan, so God allowed some of them to "test Israel" (Judges 3:4).

The most famous battle happened between Goliath, a giant Philistine warrior, and David, a shepherd boy. David killed Goliath with one stone from his sling.

David Chosen as Israel's Second King (1 Samuel 16)

God rejected Israel's first king because of Saul's pride and disobedience. Then the Lord sent the prophet Samuel to choose another king from the sons of a man named Jesse.

Samuel looked over the seven oldest sons, but God said no to each of them. "Man looks at the outward appearance," God said, "but the LORD looks at the heart" (1 Samuel 16:7). Finally, Samuel was introduced to Jesse's youngest son, David. God said to Samuel, "Arise, anoint him, for this is he" (verse 12).

Samuel poured oil over David's head, and "the Spirit of the LORD came on David from that day forward" (verse 13).

David's Rise, Saul's Fall (1 Samuel 17–31)

Over time, David's popularity with the people of Israel grew. (His victory over the Philistine giant Goliath certainly helped!) Saul, who was still king when David was anointed, became jealous. He even tried a few times to kill the young man. But David never fought back, even when he had a chance to kill Saul. He knew that Saul was God's anointed king. David wouldn't do anything until it was clearly God's time for him to be crowned (1 Samuel 26:10–11).

How Could a Shepherd Boy Defeat a Battle-Hardened Giant?

Israel was facing the Philistines in war. One of those Philistines was Goliath, who was really, *really* big—the Bible says he stood nine feet tall! His armor and weapons were all as supersized as he was. Israel's soldiers were terrified of Goliath.

Then in stepped the shepherd boy, David, wanting to fight the giant. David said he'd already killed a bear and a lion—though by God's strength, not his own (1 Samuel 17:7).

Goliath laughed at David's size. But the shepherd boy spoke up boldly, saying he was fighting in the name of the Lord (1 Samuel 17:45–46). David then loaded his sling with one of the five small rocks he'd taken from a stream. He slung it, hitting Goliath right in the forehead. The giant crashed to the ground. Then David took Goliath's own sword and chopped off his head!

David Becomes King (2 Samuel)

The book of 2 Samuel begins where 1 Samuel ends. After Saul had died in battle, David was crowned king in Judah—the southern section of Israel where Jerusalem is. He ruled there for seven years, and then he became ruler of *all* Israel for another thirty-three years. The author of 2 Samuel gives readers an honest look at David—both the great things he did and some really bad decisions he made.

David's Achievements as King (2 Samuel, 1 Chronicles 11–29)

David—Israel's greatest king—accomplished much for God and for the kingdom of Israel. He made the twelve tribes into one powerful nation, and he made Jerusalem Israel's capital city. David won lots of battles, bringing in a time of peace that allowed his son Solomon to build a temple for God. David also wrote more than seventy of the Bible's psalms.

Most important of all, though, David was known as "a man after God's own heart." He had some real problems, but David loved and served the Lord. He even became an ancestor of the Messiah, Jesus Christ!

The "Davidic Covenant"

The Davidic Covenant is a series of promises God made to David through the prophet Nathan. You can read about them in 2 Samuel 7. They're also summarized in 1 Chronicles 17:11–14 and 2 Chronicles 6:16. These promises assured David that his son Solomon would build a temple as a place of worship, that the Messiah would come from his family, and that the Messiah's kingdom would last forever. The promise was unconditional, meaning it didn't depend on David's (or Israel's) obedience. God would be faithful to His own word.

"Your house and your kingdom shall be established forever before you," God told him. "Your throne shall be established forever" (2 Samuel 7:16). This part of the promise was mysterious to David. But we know that it will be fulfilled through Jesus, when He comes to earth as King at the end of time.

David's Sin (2 Samuel 11)

David was a great leader, but he was far from perfect. One time, he saw the beautiful wife of one of his best soldiers, and he wanted her. Since he was king, he told someone to go get Bathsheba, and she came to his palace. Then David tried to hide his sin by making plans to have her husband, Uriah, killed in battle. David then married Bathsheba, but his actions "displeased the LORD" (2 Samuel 11:27). The prophet Nathan told David about his horrible sin, and the king realized how wrong he was. God forgave David, but his sin had serious consequences.

How David's Sin Affected Him and His Kingdom (2 Samuel 12)

When David confessed, Nathan assured him that God had forgiven him. David wasn't going to die right then. But Nathan also told what would happen because of David's mistake. First, his and Bathsheba's first son would die. Not only that, but David's family would suffer from violence. This prophecy was fulfilled when one of David's sons, Absalom, killed his half brother, Amnon, and then tried to take David's crown. He almost succeeded, but God stepped in for David. Joab, David's military commander, then killed Absalom against David's wishes.

How Could David Be "A Man after God's Own Heart"?

Israel's first king, Saul, did some good things. However, he also made very poor decisions that led to his downfall. First, he offered a sacrifice without God's approval (1 Samuel 13:9–14). Then he disobeyed God's order by not killing the Amalekites' king and best livestock (1 Samuel 15:3). Finally, he lied to Samuel, God's prophet, about what he had done.

That's when God decided to replace Saul (see 1 Samuel 13:14).

As it turns out, King David would also make some poor decisions—and some of them were really, really bad. But in spite of his weaknesses, David truly loved God. When he failed, he always admitted his guilt, confessed his sin, and returned to the Lord.

Solomon Becomes Israel's Third King (1 Kings 1:1–2:11)

David and Bathsheba's first baby died shortly after birth. But they soon had a second child, and David named him Solomon. God had told David that Solomon was His choice for king (1 Chronicles 22:6–10). So after Solomon was anointed, David reminded him of what would make him successful: "Do what the Lord your God tells you. Walk in His ways. Keep all His Laws and His Word, by what is written in the Law of Moses. Then you will do well in all that you do and in every place you go" (1 Kings 2:3 NLV).

Solomon's Wise Request (1 Kings 3:6–15)

Solomon had big shoes to fill. He wanted to be a great king like his father, but he wasn't sure he was able. After becoming king of Israel, Solomon saw God in a dream. The Lord said, "Ask. What shall I give you?" (1 Kings 3:5). Solomon quickly replied, "Give Your servant an understanding heart to judge Your people, that I may discern between good and bad" (verse 9). God was very pleased with that request, so He gave Solomon "a wise and understanding heart" (verse 12). . .as well as great riches and honor!

How Wise Was Solomon?

Early in his rule, Solomon's wisdom was tested by an argument between two women. One night, one of the women accidentally caused her baby's death. So she took the other woman's child as her own, starting a fight that ended up before the king.

Solomon's response? "Divide the living child in two. Give half to the one woman and half to the other" (1 Kings 3:25 NLV). Immediately, one woman cried out, "O, my lord, give her the living child. Do not kill him" (verse 26 NLV). This response told Solomon exactly who the *real* mother was!

The Bible says Solomon spoke three thousand proverbs (1 Kings 4:32), many of which are found in the book of Proverbs. Solomon also probably wrote the book of Ecclesiastes, which shows how meaningless life is without God.

Solomon's Temple (1 Kings 5–6)

When he became king, Solomon got started building a spectacular temple for God in Jerusalem. Some 180,000 people provided the materials and did the work. It took seven years to complete this worship center, which was 180 feet long, 90 feet wide, and 50 feet high at its ceiling. The highest point of the building was about 20 stories, or over 200 feet. Solomon used the best lumber, the most precious metals, and the most talented craftsmen in the world. His attitude seemed to be "Nothing but the best for God."

The Richest Ruler in the World (1 Kings 9–10)

Solomon soon became the richest and most powerful king in the world. He brought in incredible treasures from other regions of the world. Some have guessed that Solomon was worth more than two *trillion* dollars in today's money!

Israel was flying high during Solomon's reign. But the good times didn't last long. God had promised Solomon that his kingdom would last forever. . .as long as he followed God like his father, David, had. If Solomon failed, terrible things would occur (1 Kings 9:6–9).

Sadly, that's exactly what happened.

Why Do the Old Testament's Historical Books Repeat Themselves So Much?

The books of 1 Kings and 2 Kings and 1 Chronicles and 2 Chronicles contain a lot of the same information. First Chronicles describes King David's reign over Israel and ends with Solomon, David's son, taking the throne after his father's death. Second Chronicles covers more than four hundred years of history, beginning with the building of Solomon's temple and ending with the Jews' return from seventy years of captivity in Babylon.

The books of Kings cover much of the same territory. But while they focus mostly on historical events, 1 and 2 Chronicles emphasize the spiritual side of those events.

Ancient Jewish tradition says the priest Ezra wrote Chronicles after the captivity. He repeated much of what was in the books of Kings to teach the people how to worship God.

Solomon Goes Wrong (1 Kings 11:1-10)

Solomon's reign as king of Israel started well. But in later years he broke several of God's laws. He married *seven hundred* women—some of whom were Moabites, Ammonites, Edomites, Sidonians, and Hittites who worshipped false gods. Over time, Solomon even began building worship centers for their fake gods.

God Announces Judgment for Solomon's Sin (1 Kings 11:11-13)

Solomon's foolishness angered God. One day, the Lord appeared to Solomon and told him that the great kingdom of Israel would pay a heavy price for its king's sin: "Because you have done this, and you have not kept My covenant and My statutes, which I have commanded you, I will surely tear the kingdom from you and will give it to your servant. However, I will not do it in your days, for your father David's sake. But I will tear it out of the hand of your son. However, I will not tear away all of the kingdom, but will give one tribe to your son for My servant David's sake, and for Jerusalem's sake, which I have chosen" (1 Kings 11:11–13).

Solomon's "Vanity"

The book of Ecclesiastes is downright depressing!

Many Bible experts believe that Solomon wrote this book late in his life. He may have been thinking of how empty a life of wealth, power, and pleasure is without God.

If anyone understood that truth, it was Solomon. His career as Israel's third king began well, as he was fully committed to God and to His Word. But later, wealth and power and his love of women took hold of his heart. The kingdom crumbled soon after his death.

Ecclesiastes shows us how worthless life is—even a life of wealth and ease—when God isn't first in our lives. In the end, though, Solomon described what he learned about the true purpose of life: "Fear God and keep His commandments, for this is the whole duty of man. For God shall bring every work into judgment, with every secret thing, whether it is good or evil" (12:13–14).

The Kingdom Divides (1 Kings 11–12)

In 1 Kings 11:31–35, a prophet named Ahijah predicted that Israel would divide into two kingdoms. The split happened shortly after Solomon's death, as his son Rehoboam began to reign. Leaders from northern Israel were unhappy with the heavy burdens Solomon had placed on the people. But Rehoboam foolishly refused to listen (1 Kings 12:1–24). So ten northern tribes broke away, becoming a new kingdom of Israel under the leadership of Jeroboam.

Failed Leadership in the North and the South (1 Kings 12–14)

Under Jeroboam's terrible leadership, the northern kingdom of Israel started worshipping idols. The king was afraid that his people would travel to Jerusalem to worship God at the temple and then might lose their loyalty to him. So he built two golden idols, one in the north and one in the south of the country.

Rehoboam also failed as a leader in the southern kingdom of Judah. His father, Solomon, had built a beautiful temple to honor God. But during Rehoboam's reign, the people angered God by following false gods and doing many other bad things (1 Kings 14:22–24). Rehoboam did nothing to bring his people back to the one true God.

Elijah

Elijah lived during the ninth century BC, after David and Solomon's Israel had split in two. He was one of the greatest prophets in Jewish history. Elijah worked to lead the people of the northern kingdom of Israel away from the false god Baal and back to the one true God. So people could know he truly spoke for God, Elijah performed many miracles.

His most dramatic miracle came when he challenged 450 prophets of Baal at Mount Carmel (1 Kings 18:17–40). These false prophets called on Baal all day long, begging him to send fire from heaven. But nothing happened. Then Elijah built a stone altar, put an animal sacrifice on a pile of wood, and soaked everything with water. When he prayed, God sent fire from heaven to burn everything—even the water!

A New Prophet, Old Problems (2 Kings)

Second Kings begins with Elijah going up to heaven in a chariot of fire. Then his helper, Elisha, became Israel's leading prophet. The book also describes how the northern kingdom fell to the Assyrians around 722 BC (chapters 16–17) and how the southern kingdom was conquered by the Babylonians around 585 BC (chapters 24–25). In between are stories about the various kings of Israel and Judah. Most of them did a very bad job.

Where the Northern Kingdom Went Wrong (2 Kings 1–17)

None of Israel's kings followed God or encouraged His people to do so. One of the worst was Ahab, who led the people to worship the false god Baal. Second Kings 17:7–17 gives a sad summary of the sins of the leaders and people of Israel. They worshipped false gods, practiced witchcraft, and "turned away from [God's] Laws and His agreement which He made with their fathers" (2 Kings 17:15 NLV).

Elijah and Elisha

Elijah is one of two people in the Bible who never died. (The other was a man named Enoch, described in Genesis 5.) Elijah was taken to heaven in a "chariot of fire" on a whirlwind (2 Kings 2:11–12). Elisha realized it was time to take Elijah's job, so he made a special request of Elijah before he left: "I ask, let a double portion of your spirit be upon me" (2 Kings 2:9). That's exactly what happened!

Like Elijah, Elisha became a powerful prophet of God who performed many miracles. Second Kings 2–13 tells of well over a dozen miracles (including prophecies). Some examples: parting the waters of the Jordan River (2:14), providing water for the army of Israel (3:16–25), raising a boy from the dead (4:18–37), and curing the Syrian army commander Naaman of leprosy (5:1–19).

Israel Warned of Judgment (2 Kings, Prophetic Books)

God had warned the people of Israel over and over to turn away from their idolatry and back to Him. Elijah and Elisha both urged the people of the northern kingdom to repent. The Old Testament prophetic books Hosea (13:16) and Micah (1:6) predicted the destruction of Samaria, the capital of the northern kingdom. The prophet Amos also predicted the destruction of the northern kingdom of Israel. Isaiah prophesied that God would use the Assyrian Empire to punish Israel for its idolatry (Isaiah 10:5–19).

The Northern Kingdom Invaded (2 Kings 15–18)

Beginning around 733 BC, the Assyrian king Tiglath-pileser invaded the northern region of Israel and took many people captive (2 Kings 15:29). In 721 BC, another Assyrian king, Shalmaneser, attacked Samaria, Israel's capital. Samaria fell three years later (2 Kings 18:9–12).

The Assyrians

Assyria was a large kingdom located between the Euphrates and Tigris rivers. The Assyrians worshipped false gods and did terrible things to the people they conquered. Several Old Testament prophets spoke out against them.

God called the famous prophet Jonah to preach to Nineveh, the capital city of Assyria (Jonah 1:1–3). At first, Jonah said, "No way!" But after spending some time in the belly of a large fish, he got up and gave God's warning to the city. When the king and his people repented, God turned His anger from Nineveh—for a while, at least (Jonah 3:10).

In 701 BC, the Assyrians set their sights on Jerusalem. Hezekiah, a godly king, prayed for help—and God promised him that the Assyrians would never set foot inside the city (Isaiah 37:33). In one night, God killed 185,000 Assyrian forces (Isaiah 37:36). Their king, Sennacherib, returned to Nineveh, where his own sons killed him as he worshipped his god Nisroch (Isaiah 37:38).

Around 612 BC, the Medes, Babylonians, and Scythians joined together and attacked Nineveh, bringing an end to the Assyrian Empire.

The Southern Kingdom Continues (2 Kings, 2 Chronicles)

The rulers of the southern Jewish kingdom of Judah were Rehoboam, Abijah, Asa, Jehoshaphat, Jehoram (or Joram), Ahaziah, Athaliah (the only ruling queen), Joash (or Jehoash), Amaziah, Uzziah (or Azariah), Jotham, Ahaz, Hezekiah, Manasseh, Amon, Josiah, Jehoahaz, Jehoiakim, Jehoiachin, and Zedekiah. Compared to Israel's kings, Judah's rulers were slightly better. Even then, only about a third did well. And some of them made serious mistakes at one time or another.

Judah Declines (2 Kings, 2 Chronicles)

After the death of Josiah, Judah's last good king, a series of ungodly, wicked kings ruled Judah: Jehoahaz (609 BC), Jehoiakim (609–597 BC), Jehoiachin (597 BC), and Zedekiah (597–586 BC). None of these men loved or served God. Under their leadership, the people of the southern kingdom slipped into idol worship and disobedience.

Because the people of Judah ignored God's prophets, God sent judgment on Judah several decades after Israel's fall.

Hezekiah

Hezekiah was the thirteenth king of Judah. He began his reign at age twenty-five and ruled for twenty-nine years (about 715 to 686 BC). Hezekiah was the son of an evil king, Ahaz—but he was nothing like his father. Hezekiah was one of the few kings of Judah who served God well. He is considered the best king in Judah's history.

Hezekiah's story is found in 2 Kings 16:20–20:21 and 2 Chronicles 28:27–32:33. One interesting part of his story involves a miraculous healing. At age thirty-nine, King Hezekiah became so ill that the prophet Isaiah told him to get ready to die. But Hezekiah asked for God's mercy to live longer. Before Isaiah had even left the palace, God told him to tell the king that his prayers had been heard. God gave Hezekiah another fifteen years to live (2 Kings 20:1–11)!

Prophets Warn of Judgment on Judah (2 Chronicles 35–36, Jeremiah, Etc.)

God sent many prophets to warn the people of Judah that judgment was coming. Jeremiah was one of the "major prophets"—which means the book he wrote was longer than those of the "minor prophets." Jeremiah shared largely bad news. God had given the people warning after warning through earlier prophets, but they hadn't listened. Now, destruction was coming to Jerusalem.

God also spoke to Judah through the prophets Isaiah, Joel, Micah, Habakkuk, and Zephaniah.

The Fall of Judah (2 Kings 24–25, 2 Chronicles 36)

After warning Judah for so many years, God finally ran out of patience. He sent the Babylonian Empire to punish His people. Babylonian soldiers came against Judah and Jerusalem in three different waves. In the first two, they captured many of Judah's bright young people (including a man named Daniel) and the king, Jehoiachin, and took them away to Babylon. But in the third wave (around 586 BC), they destroyed Jerusalem and its walls, knocked down the temple, and carried all the temple's treasures back to Babylon (2 Kings 24:13).

How Could God Use Evil People to Accomplish His Plans?

The Old Testament prophet Habakkuk understood that God had to punish Judah for its wickedness and rebellion. But why in the world, he wondered, would God use the evil Babylonians to do it?

As the all-knowing Creator and Keeper of the universe, God can and will do as He pleases. He has the right to choose whatever methods He wants.

Habakkuk's reaction (1:12–13) shows that God isn't offended when His people ask Him what He is doing. But we must always remember two things: (1) He's God and we're not, and (2) He doesn't owe us an answer. It's our job to trust that He has everything under control.

MAIN ROAD

Jerusalem after the Babylonian Attacks (Jeremiah, Lamentations)

When Jeremiah saw the result of the Babylonian attacks, it broke his heart. He poured out his sadness in the book of Lamentations.

Jeremiah knew the destruction of Jerusalem was the result of the people's sin and rebellion: "[The Lord] has destroyed without pity. He has caused those who hate you to have joy over you. He has given strength to those who fight against you" (Lamentations 2:17 NLV). The book of Lamentations shows why Jeremiah is often called the "Weeping Prophet."

Hope despite the Destruction (Jeremiah, Lamentations)

You won't find a happy ending in Lamentations. But that doesn't mean all hope was lost. Despite all the destruction, God also gave these words of hope and restoration: "See, I will make it well again, and I will heal them. I will let them have much peace and truth. I will return the land to Judah and to Israel, and I will help them to become as they were before. I will make them clean from all the sins they have done against Me. I will forgive all their sins against Me" (Jeremiah 33:6–8 NLV).

Nebuchadnezzar

Nebuchadnezzar was king of Babylon from around 605 to 562 BC. Under him, the Babylonian Empire became one of the most powerful kingdoms in the world. It was also filled with impressive buildings and art.

In the Bible, Nebuchadnezzar is best known for conquering Judah, destroying Jerusalem, and carrying its residents to Babylon.

Daniel 3 says Nebuchadnezzar built a golden statue (probably of himself). Then he ordered all the people to bow down to it whenever music was played. In chapter 4, Daniel interpreted a dream for Nebuchadnezzar, telling the king that he should humble himself. Nebuchadnezzar ignored him. . .and was driven insane for seven years!

When he regained his mind, Nebuchadnezzar declared of God, "How great are His signs! And how mighty are His wonders! His kingdom is an everlasting kingdom, and His authority is from generation to generation" (Daniel 4:3).

Jewish Life in Babylon (Jeremiah 29)

In their three attacks, the Babylonians took many thousands of Judah's smartest and most talented people to Babylon. Thankfully, they treated them fairly well. The Jews lived in towns and villages along the Chebar River and were allowed to raise their families, farm, and make a living. Jeremiah had encouraged the people to marry, have children, and build homes while they lived in Babylon.

The Fall of the Babylonian Empire (Daniel 5)

Babylon is where Daniel and Ezekiel prophesied. Both men had been taken from Jerusalem when Nebuchadnezzar's forces attacked Judah. Daniel did very well in Babylon, even becoming an advisor to the Babylonians, and later, the Persians.

In Daniel 2, Daniel explained that King Nebuchadnezzar's dream predicted the fall of Babylon. (Isaiah also described this in chapters 13, 14, and 21.) Daniel also predicted the rise of the Medes and Persians, in chapter 5.

This came true in 539 BC, when the Persian king Cyrus the Great conquered Babylon.

God's Prophets in Babylon

Ezekiel was one of the many people carried off to Babylon after the invasion of Jerusalem. He preached that even though God had judged the people of Judah, He would also forgive them and bring them back to their land.

Daniel also lived during the captivity. Though he was surrounded by people who didn't know God, he remained faithful. He wrote down his prophecies and experiences while longing for the land of Judah. Daniel wrote, "In the first year of Darius. . .I, Daniel, understood by the books the number of the years, of which the word of the LORD came to Jeremiah the prophet, that He would complete seventy years in the desolations of Jerusalem" (Daniel 9:1–2).

God Fulfills His Promise (Ezra 1)

Though the book of Ezra comes before the books of the prophets in the Bible, it takes place around the same time. Ezra begins with what is called "the Edict of Cyrus." (Cyrus was king of Persia, the empire that conquered the Babylonians in 539 BC.) In this ruling, Cyrus allowed the Jews to return to Judah. This fulfilled God's promise to bring them back after seventy years of captivity. Because of his kindness and respect toward them, Cyrus is respected by Jews to this day.

Three Waves of Returnees (Ezra, Nehemiah)

After Cyrus' order, three waves of Jews traveled nine hundred miles from Babylon to Judah. The first wave was led by Zerubbabel, and they rebuilt the altar and the foundation for a new temple. Some eighty years later, around 458 BC, the priest Ezra led a second wave of Jews to Jerusalem. When his group arrived, they began to restore the old ways of worshipping God. Then around 445 BC, Nehemiah led the third wave of Jews to Jerusalem. Their main job was to rebuild the walls of the city.

Esther

Esther was a beautiful young Jewish girl who lived in Persia, along with about a million other Jews. She probably lived between the first and second waves of Jews returning to Jerusalem. Esther was the wife of King Ahasuerus (called Xerxes in some Bible translations), making her queen of Persia.

When Esther's cousin and foster father Mordecai told her of a plot to murder every Jew in Persia, she risked her own life to save them. In the end, King Ahasuerus allowed the Jews to fight back against their enemies. The plot was the idea of a selfish Persian official named Haman. In the end, the king had Haman hanged.

Surprisingly, Esther's story never mentions God. But He's clearly a big part of the story. God was working behind the scenes to save His people and continue their mission to bless the whole world.

Finishing the Temple (Haggai, Zechariah)

Many Jews had returned to Jerusalem. But they were slow to build a new temple to replace the one the Babylonians had destroyed years before. They laid a foundation but then stopped when their enemies threatened them.

But through the prophet Haggai, God declared, "Is it a time for you yourselves to live in your houses with walls covered with wood, while [the temple] lies waste?" (Haggai 1:4 NLV). And the prophet Zechariah carried this message from the Lord: "Let your hands be strong for building the Lord's house" (Zechariah 8:9 NLV).

Urged on by the prophets, the governor Zerubbabel started the work again. This second temple was completed in about four years, in 516 BC.

God's Final Old Testament Words (Malachi)

The book of Malachi was written for Jews in Jerusalem about a hundred years after the Babylonian captivity. The people thought they were pleasing God, but their hearts were far from Him. So God demanded they correct their attitudes. After Malachi closed out the Old Testament, God wouldn't speak through any prophets again for four hundred years. This silence was broken when John the Baptist announced the Messiah had arrived. . .and the New Testament era began!

SIDE ROAD

"Oddball" Prophets

The Old Testament includes three prophetic books not addressed to Israel or Judah. One, the very short book of Obadiah, warns of judgment on Edom for fighting against Israel and bragging about it.

The second, the book of Jonah, tells of a disobedient prophet who tried to run from God. The Lord called Jonah to warn Nineveh, a wicked Assyrian city, of His judgment. Jonah was then thrown off his ship during a violent storm and swallowed by a giant fish. When he came to his senses and prayed, God had the fish spit Jonah onto the shore. Then Jonah went to Nineveh and fulfilled God's mission. Everyone, including the king of Nineveh, turned away from their sin. God spared the city. . .at least for a time.

About 150 years later, the book of Nahum shows that the Assyrians had forgotten God's kindness and mercy. They were filled with pride, violence, and idol worship, even worse than they had been before. "Woe to the bloody city!" God cried (Nahum 3:1).

MAIN ROAD

The Old Testament Hints of the Messiah (Genesis 3:15)

You won't find Jesus' name in the Old Testament, but that part of the Bible is really all about Him! It tells the story of how God worked throughout human history to prepare the world for its Messiah. After Adam and Eve disobeyed Him in Eden, God gave the first hint of His plan of salvation. The Lord told Satan, "I will make you and the woman hate each other, and your seed and her seed will hate each other. He will crush your head, and you will crush his heel" (Genesis 3:15 NLV).

The Old Testament Predicts the Messiah (Psalms, Prophets)

Through the history of God's chosen people, the Lord spoke through many men to give the Jews promises of a coming Messiah. The Old Testament made predictions about the Messiah's birth (Isaiah 7:14; Micah 5:2), His parables (Psalm 78:1–2), His miracles (Isaiah 35:5–6), the suffering and death He endured for His people (Isaiah 53), His resurrection from the dead (Psalm 118:17–18), and much more. Some scholars count more than three hundred predictions!

SIDE ROAD

Isaiah—the "Fifth Gospel"

The first four books of the New Testament—Matthew, Mark, Luke, and John—contain the story of Jesus' life. Together, they are called the *"Gospels"*—a word meaning "good news."

The Old Testament book of Isaiah was written around seven hundred years before Jesus' birth. It contains so many prophecies of the coming Messiah that some Christians have called it the "fifth Gospel." Almost one-third of Isaiah's 66 chapters contain prophecies about the birth, life, and death of Jesus Christ, or about His return to earth in the end times.

Isaiah's best-known prophecy says Jesus "was hurt for our wrong-doing. He was crushed for our sins. He was punished so we would have peace. He was beaten so we would be healed. All of us like sheep have gone the wrong way. Each of us has turned to his own way. And the Lord has put on Him the sin of us all" (53:5–6 NLV).

Isaiah 56:8 hints that this salvation wouldn't be just for Israelites but also for non-Jews. That prophecy was fulfilled when Jesus' apostles—including Peter and Paul—began preaching to the Gentiles.

The "Annunciation" of Jesus' Birth (Luke 1:26–38)

Of the four Gospels, only Matthew and Luke say anything about Jesus' birth. Matthew wrote that Jesus' mother, Mary, "was found with child from the Holy Spirit" (1:18). Luke, who was also a doctor, gives more detail. He reports that the angel Gabriel appeared to Mary, telling her that she would soon give birth to the Son of God. This would fulfill Isaiah's prophecy: "A young woman, who has never had a man, will give birth to a son. She will give Him the name Immanuel" (Isaiah 7:14 NLV).

Mary and Joseph Guided to Bethlehem (Luke 2:1–21)

Mary and Joseph lived in the town of Nazareth. But Micah had predicted that the village of Bethlehem would be the Savior's birthplace (Micah 5:2). So God made sure Mary and Joseph were in Bethlehem when Jesus was born. He used the Roman emperor Caesar Augustus, who ordered all Jews in Israel to travel to their families' hometowns to sign up for a census.

Many people were already there for the census, so the couple couldn't find a place to stay the night. So they stayed in a place where animals were kept. . .and that's where Jesus was born. After His birth, Mary and Joseph laid Him in a manger—a food box for livestock.

Women in Jesus' Genealogy

The Gospels include two genealogies (family trees) of Jesus Christ—Matthew 1:1–17 and Luke 3:23–38. Matthew mentions four Old Testament women in Jesus' family line: Tamar (1:3), Rahab (1:5), Ruth (1:5), and Bathsheba, "the wife of Uriah" (1:6). Two of these women (Rahab and Ruth) were not Israelites, and all four had messy lives. Yet God used them to bring Jesus into the world.

In Genesis, the Bible's first book, God told Abraham, "Look now toward heaven and count the stars, if you are able to number them. . . . So shall your descendants be" (Genesis 15:5). God also told Abraham that "in you shall all families of the earth be blessed" (Genesis 12:3). Why? Because his family line would produce Jesus, the Messiah!

Angels Announce Jesus' Birth (Luke 2:8–20)

In a field outside Bethlehem, shepherds watched over their sheep. Suddenly, an angel of God appeared and announced Jesus' birth. The shepherds were terrified! But the angel told them, "Do not be afraid. See! I bring you good news of great joy which is for all people. Today, One Who saves from the punishment of sin has been born in the city of David. He is Christ the Lord. . . . You will find the Baby with cloth around Him, lying in a place where cattle are fed" (Luke 2:10–12 NLV). The shepherds hurried into town and found exactly what the angel had said.

Jesus' Life Is Threatened (Matthew 2)

Within about two years of His birth, Jesus was visited by "wise men" who brought gifts. Also called magi, these men were from "the east"—probably Persia (modern-day Iran), hundreds of miles away. They had "seen His star in the East" and come to worship the "King of the Jews" (Matthew 2:2).

King Herod didn't like that report. He thought a "King of the Jews" was a threat to his own rule. So after the wise men left Bethlehem, an angel warned Joseph at night to run to Egypt to escape Herod's anger (Matthew 2:13).

Joseph obeyed immediately. He and his family then stayed in Egypt until Herod died. This fulfilled another Old Testament prophecy: "Out of Egypt I have called My Son" (Matthew 2:15; Hosea 11:1).

Jesus' Childhood

The Bible gives us just a few details of Jesus' childhood.

When Jesus was only a few days old, His parents brought Him to the temple for dedication. There, a godly man named Simeon met Jesus, Mary, and Joseph. The Lord had promised Simeon that he would meet the Messiah. And at that moment, the Spirit told Simeon that this was the Savior he had been longing for (Luke 2:25–35).

At age twelve, Jesus attended His first Passover in Jerusalem ...where He proved how unique He truly was (Luke 2:41–51). As His family began their journey back to Nazareth, Jesus separated from them. (Imagine how upset Mary and Joseph must have been when they realized they'd "lost" the Son of God!) But after three days of searching, they found Jesus at the temple, discussing the law with Jewish teachers. Luke 2:47 says that "all who heard Him were astonished at His understanding and answers."

John the Baptist Prepares Jesus' Way (John 1:15–37)

John the Baptist was the first prophet sent by God since Malachi, about four hundred years earlier. John came to tell other people about Jesus (John 1:7) and called people to repent, or turn from, their sins.

One day, John saw Jesus walking by. John cried out, "Behold, the Lamb of God who takes away the sin of the world" (John 1:29). During Old Testament times, people had to sacrifice a pure, innocent lamb to cover their sins. John's words told the purpose of Jesus' life on earth.

John Baptizes Jesus (Matthew 3:13–17)

Before Jesus began teaching in public, He traveled to the Jordan River. John was there baptizing people who had turned from their sins. Jesus had never sinned, but He still asked John to baptize Him "to fulfill all righteousness" (Matthew 3:15). As Jesus came up out of the water, the Spirit of God floated down on Him "like a dove." A voice from heaven said, "This is My beloved Son, in whom I am well pleased" (Matthew 3:17).

John the Baptist: Miracle Baby

The Old Testament describes several miraculous births—including those of Isaac, Samson, and Samuel. In the New Testament, we find another one: the birth of John the Baptist.

His parents—Zechariah and Elizabeth—were old and had been unable to have a child. One day as Zechariah served in the temple, the angel Gabriel appeared. He said, "Do not be afraid. Your prayer has been heard. Your wife Elizabeth will give birth to a son. You are to name him John. . . . He will turn the hearts of the fathers back to their children. He will teach those who do not obey to be right with God. He will get people ready for the Lord" (Luke 1:13, 17 NLV).

Zechariah couldn't believe it—and he lost his voice for a while as punishment. Several months later, just as Gabriel had promised, Elizabeth had a son. He was called John, and we know him today as John the Baptist. Shortly before Jesus started His ministry, John started preparing people for the Messiah.

The Devil Tempts Jesus (Matthew 4:1–11, Luke 4:1–13)

Right after Jesus was baptized, the Holy Spirit led Him into the desert. There He prayed and went without food for forty days. The devil wanted to ruin the Messiah's mission. So he tempted Jesus to do three things: turn stones into bread, jump from the top of the temple and rely on angels to break His fall, and worship Satan in return for all the kingdoms of the world. Jesus responded each time by quoting scripture (see Matthew 4:4, 7, 10). After the third temptation, the devil ran away.

Jesus Calls His Disciples (Matthew 4:19–26, Mark 1:16–20, Luke 5:1–11)

The devil's temptations couldn't stop Jesus' mission. He soon began to call a group of twelve "disciples" (learners) to travel with Him: Peter and his brother Andrew, James and his brother John, Philip, Bartholomew (or Nathanael), Matthew, Thomas, James the son of Alphaeus, Simon the Zealot, Thaddaeus, and Judas Iscariot. Jesus wanted these men to follow Him, learn from Him, and then take His message of salvation to the world as "apostles" (sent ones).

Peter and Andrew were fishermen, but Jesus told them, "Follow Me, and I will make you fishers of men" (Matthew 4:19). Soon, they'd be catching people for God!

Why Would God Allow Jesus to Be Tempted?

Matthew 4:1 says, "Jesus was led up *by the Spirit* into the wilderness to be tempted by the devil" (emphasis added).

But why would God allow His beloved Son to face such a hard trial? The writer of Hebrews explains: "Our Religious Leader understands how weak we are. Christ was tempted in every way we are tempted, but He did not sin" (4:15 NLV).

As a member of the Trinity (Father, Son, and Holy Spirit), Jesus is the eternal God. He took on human form so that He could fully understand His creation. Then He faced temptation so that He could feel our struggles. And, by using the powerful weapon of the Bible against the devil's attacks (see Ephesians 6:13, 17), Jesus set an example for us.

The Sermon on the Mount (Matthew 5–7)

One day, Jesus taught a large crowd gathered by the Sea of Galilee. It was near the small fishing town of Capernaum, which He had made His home. From the hillside, Jesus preached what is called the Sermon on the Mount. He began with a list of nine statements of blessing, which came to be known as the *Beatitudes*—a Latin term meaning "blessed," "happy," or "fortunate." From there, Jesus taught about tough subjects such as the law, marriage, divorce, judging others, false teaching, and other important topics.

The Sermon on the Plain (Luke 6:20–49)

The Gospel of Luke contains a passage that some believe is a different account of the Sermon on the Mount—but others think it's a "Sermon on the Plain" that He preached at a different time. It begins with a similar list of beatitudes and follows with some words of Jesus that overlap with Matthew's account. Even if the two accounts are of different sermons, Jesus' main points are the same.

The Lord's Prayer

During His Sermon on the Mount, Jesus gave a beautiful model for prayer, which came to be called "the Lord's Prayer":

> *"Our Father who is in heaven, hallowed be Your name.*
>
> *Your kingdom come. Your will be done on earth as it is in heaven.*
>
> *Give us this day our daily bread.*
>
> *And forgive us our debts, as we forgive our debtors.*
>
> *And do not lead us into temptation, but deliver us from evil.*
>
> *For Yours is the kingdom and the power and the glory forever. Amen."*

MATTHEW 6:9–13

Many people memorize the Lord's Prayer and recite it word for word. Others believe it's more of a model for how to pray—telling us how we should praise God and follow His will.

Jesus' Ministry of Healing (Matthew 8)

The Gospels tell us Jesus healed all kinds of people—men, women, children, Jews, and Gentiles—of many problems and diseases. This fulfilled Old Testament prophecies such as Isaiah 35:5–6: "Then the eyes of the blind shall be opened, and the ears of the deaf shall be unstopped. Then the lame man shall leap as a deer, and the tongue of the mute shall sing, for waters shall break out in the wilderness, and streams in the desert." But Jesus also said He performed such miracles so that people could know that "the Father is in Me and I in Him" (John 10:38).

Jesus Shows His Power over Death (Luke 7–8, John 11)

While He was on earth, Jesus proved His power over the weather, evil spirits, disease, and even death. The Bible tells the stories of three people brought back to life by Jesus: the son of a widow who lived in the village of Nain (Luke 7:11–17), the 12-year-old daughter of a synagogue leader in Capernaum (Luke 8:40–56), and His friend Lazarus of Bethany, who had been in the grave for four days (John 11:1–44).

SIDE ROAD

Seven "I Ams" of Jesus

In the Gospel of John, Jesus makes seven "I am" statements that show who He really is:

- ▶ "I am the bread of life" (John 6:35).
- ▶ "I am the light of the world" (John 8:12).
- ▶ "I am the door of the sheep" (John 10:7).
- ▶ "I am the good shepherd" (John 10:11).
- ▶ "I am the resurrection and the life" (John 11:25).
- ▶ "I am the way, the truth, and the life" (John 14:6).
- ▶ "I am the true vine" (John 15:1).

Another time, Jesus used only the words "I am" in response to a question from Jewish leaders who hated Him. See more on page 110.

Jesus Feeds Five Thousand People (Matthew 14:31–21, Mark 6:30–44, Luke 9:10–17, John 6:1–14)

Huge crowds followed Jesus. Some did because they were interested in His teaching. Others just wanted food or healing.

One evening, Jesus told His disciples that the crowd needed to eat. But He didn't send the people away to find food for themselves. Instead, Jesus multiplied a small amount of food—five loaves of bread and two small fish—into enough for five thousand men, plus all the women and children with them. John's Gospel notes that the people said, "This is truly that Prophet who should come into the world" (6:14).

Jesus Calms a Storm (Matthew 14:22–35, Mark 6:45–53, John 6:15–21)

Jesus then told His disciples to get in their boat and cross the Sea of Galilee. He would stay behind to pray.

As the disciples were crossing the water, a violent storm arose. But that's when they saw Jesus. . .walking on the water! When Jesus reached the disciples, He called out, "Be of good cheer. It is I. Do not be afraid" (Mark 6:50). When He climbed into the boat, the wind immediately stopped. The Gospel writer Mark says the disciples were "greatly amazed" (6:51), even though they had just seen the miracle of the feeding of the five thousand.

Why Were the Disciples So Slow to Believe?

After Jesus had calmed the storm on the Sea of Galilee, the disciples didn't know what to think. Mark 6:52 (NLV) says, "They had not learned what they should have learned from the loaves because their hearts were hard." That means they were not yet ready to understand exactly who Jesus was—even though He was performing stunning miracles in front of them.

Jesus' disciples may have expected Him to be a conquering king who would deliver Israel from its Roman rulers. But as their hearts softened, they began to see Jesus as He truly was—the Son of God who would suffer and die for human sin then rise again to prove His power over death.

Jesus Faces Religious Opposition (Matthew 9)

Many who saw Jesus' miracles were amazed and began following Him. But the Pharisees—Jewish religious leaders—weren't so impressed. When He claimed to have the authority to forgive sins (Matthew 9:3–6), they accused Him of blasphemy—of insulting God. And they said His ability to cast out evil spirits came from "the prince of the demons" (9:34). Because so many people were following Him, the Pharisees thought Jesus was a threat to their own popularity.

Jesus, a Friend of Sinners (Matthew 9:9–13, 11:18–19; Mark 2:13–20)

The Pharisees criticized Jesus for spending time with "sinners." They felt that many people—for example, tax collectors—weren't worthy of God's mercy. After all, the tax collectors worked for the Roman government and often cheated their fellow Jews. But when Jesus called a tax collector named Matthew, he immediately left his booth and became a disciple. Jesus told the complaining Pharisees, "Those who are healthy do not need a physician, but those who are sick. But go and learn what this means: 'I will have mercy and not sacrifice.' For I have come to call not the righteous but sinners to repentance" (Matthew 9:12–13).

Were There Any Good Pharisees?

Even though most Pharisees hated Jesus, Nicodemus and Joseph of Arimathea didn't. Nicodemus is best known for his late-night conversation with Jesus in John 3, when Jesus summed up the Gospel: "For God so loved the world that He gave His only begotten Son, that whoever believes in Him should not perish but have everlasting life" (John 3:16).

Joseph of Arimathea was with the Jewish religious leaders who had called for Jesus' crucifixion. But he stood against the decision because he was a secret follower of Jesus (Luke 23:51).

After Jesus' crucifixion, Nicodemus and Joseph worked together to bury His body.

Jesus Speaks in Parables (Luke 15)

Psalm 78:2 says, "I will open my mouth in a parable; I will utter dark sayings of old." The Gospel writer Matthew saw this as a prophecy of Jesus' ministry (Matthew 13:35). At least forty different times, Jesus taught through parables—simple stories that made important points about God's love and mercy, obedience toward the Lord, forgiveness, the kingdom of heaven, and God's understanding of our hearts. Jesus knew that a story is the best way for a message to enter someone's mind.

Jesus Praises Then Scolds Peter
(Matthew 16:13–20, Mark 8:27–33)

People had all sorts of opinions about who Jesus was. That's why Jesus asked His twelve disciples, "But who do you say that I am?" Peter answered correctly, "You are the Christ" (Mark 8:29). Jesus replied, "Blessed are you . . .for flesh and blood has not revealed it to you, but My Father who is in heaven" (Matthew 16:17). But when Jesus later told the disciples that He would suffer, die, and rise from the dead, Peter tried to correct his Lord. Jesus responded, "Get behind Me, Satan! For you appreciate not the things that are of God but the things that are of men" (Mark 8:33).

SIDE ROAD

Pride versus Humility

In a parable about a Pharisee and a tax collector (Luke 18:9–14), Jesus showed the different attitudes of two men who had gone to the temple to pray. When the religious leader prayed, he boasted of his own holiness. He even told God that he was better than the tax collector across the room!

The other man had a very different approach. He wouldn't even lift his eyes toward heaven. He just pounded his chest, crying out, "God, be merciful to me, a sinner" (Luke 18:13).

One of those men left the temple right before God, Jesus said—and it wasn't the Pharisee. Jesus said, "Everyone who exalts himself shall be humbled, and he who humbles himself shall be exalted" (Luke 18:14).

Jesus Transfigured (Matthew 17:1–13, Mark 9:2–13, Luke 9:28–36)

Not long before Jesus was arrested, tried, and crucified, He took His three closest disciples—Peter, James, and John—up a mountainside to pray. While Jesus prayed, His appearance changed. His face shone and His clothing turned a dazzling white. Two Old Testament people—Moses and Elijah—appeared and talked with Jesus about the trials He would soon go through. These were two of the most important men in Israel's history: Moses gave God's laws to His people, and Elijah was one of the nation's greatest prophets.

Moses and Elijah both stood for the Old Testament scriptures. . .which all point toward Jesus!

The Greatest Commandments (Matthew 22:15–40)

One day, an expert in the law of Moses tried to trick Jesus. The man asked Him which was the most important commandment. Jesus replied, "'You shall love the Lord your God with all your heart, and with all your soul, and with all your mind.' This is the first and great commandment. And the second is like it: 'You shall love your neighbor as yourself.' On these two commandments hang all the Law and the Prophets" (Matthew 22:37–40). Jesus had summed up the Ten Commandments, which break down into the way we approach God (commandments 1–4) and treat our fellow man (commandments 5–10).

SIDE ROAD

An Eighth "I Am" of Jesus

Jewish religious leaders loved throwing questions at Jesus. They hoped to trip Him up so they could accuse Him of breaking God's law. When Jesus said that Abraham "rejoiced to see My day" (John 8:56), they couldn't believe their ears. "You are not yet fifty years old," they responded, "and have You seen Abraham?" (verse 57).

Then Jesus dropped a bombshell: "Truly, truly, I say to you, before Abraham was, I am" (John 8:58). Since God had used the name "I AM" to identify Himself to Moses centuries earlier (Exodus 3:14), Jesus was claiming to be equal to God. The Jewish leaders were furious!

Jesus was much more than a great teacher or miracle worker. He was God Himself in the flesh.

Jesus' Ultimate Mission (Luke 13:22–35)

Jesus spent about three years walking around the land of Israel—teaching His disciples, performing miracles, and showing people what God's love really looks like. But Jesus had one ultimate mission on earth: to die on a Roman cross to pay for humanity's sins. That's why, during Passover week in Jerusalem, He said, "I must go on My way today and tomorrow and the day after. One who speaks for God cannot die except at Jerusalem" (Luke 13:33 NLV).

The "Triumphal Entry" (Matthew 21:1–11, Mark 11:1–11, Luke 19:28–44, John 12:12–19)

The Sunday before Jesus was crucified, He rode into Jerusalem on the back of a borrowed young donkey. This fulfilled a prophecy in Zechariah 9:9: "Rejoice greatly, O daughter of Zion; shout, O daughter of Jerusalem. Behold, your King comes to you. He is just and has salvation, lowly, and riding on a donkey, and on a colt, the foal of a donkey." As Jesus entered the city, people lined the roadway, spreading their coats and palm tree branches ahead of Him. They shouted, "Blessed is the King who comes in the name of the Lord. Peace in heaven and glory in the highest" (Luke 19:36). Christians now call this event the "Triumphal Entry."

SIDE ROAD

"Passion Week"

Jesus' "Passion Week" is described in Matthew 21–27, Mark 11–15, Luke 19–23, and John 12–19. The Gospels record several important events during this week (see Matthew 24:1–25:46, Mark 13:1–37, Luke 21:5–36). At the end of the week, Jesus met with His disciples for the Passover meal—an event known as the "Last Supper" (Matthew 26:17–30, Mark 14:12–26, Luke 22:7–38). And after the Last Supper, Jesus led His disciples to the garden of Gethsemane to pray (Matthew 26:36–56, Mark 14:32–52, Luke 22:40–53, John 18:1–11). Then He was arrested and questioned by the chief priests, the Roman governor Pontius Pilate, and King Herod (Luke 22:54–23:25).

The Last Supper (Matthew 26:17–30, Mark 14:12–26, Luke 22:7–38)

On the night Jesus was arrested, He met with His disciples for a final Passover meal together. In these last hours with His much-loved followers, Jesus established a new covenant between God and people (Luke 22:20). And He prayed His "High Priestly Prayer" (John 17) to encourage and strengthen the men. He also taught the disciples an important lesson about love, humility, and serving by washing their feet (John 13:1–17). And that night, Jesus singled out the disciple who would betray Him—Judas Iscariot (John 13:27).

Jesus' Arrest and Trial (Matthew 26–27, Mark 14–15, Luke 22–23, John 18–19)

Judas Iscariot agreed to betray Jesus for thirty pieces of silver (Matthew 26:14–16). With his help, the Jewish religious leaders captured Jesus in the garden of Gethsemane. He didn't resist; instead, He remained perfectly quiet.

The chief priests, elders, and teachers of the law questioned Jesus, asking Him if He was the Messiah. Jesus broke His silence to say, "I am" (Mark 14:62). The accusers said Jesus was guilty of blasphemy and sentenced Him to death. But they couldn't execute anyone. So they tied Jesus up and led Him to the Roman governor, Pontius Pilate.

What Part Did Pilate Play in Jesus' Death?

Pontius Pilate was the Roman governor of Judea during Jesus' arrest, trial, and crucifixion. He's the man who finally approved Jesus' crucifixion. Pilate didn't have anything against Jesus—in fact, he thought Jesus was innocent and tried several times to save His life. At one point, he even said, "What evil has He done? I have found no cause for death in Him. I will therefore chastise Him and let Him go" (Luke 23:22). But the crowd was stubborn, and Pilate gave in to their demands. He allowed Jesus to be killed (verse 24).

Jesus Is Crucified (Matthew 27:2–56, Mark 15:33–41, Luke 23:27–56, John 1:16–36)

Before Jesus was put on the cross, John 19:2–3 (NLV) says the soldiers "put a crown of thorns on His head. They put a purple coat on Him. Then they said, 'Hello, King of the Jews!' and hit Him with their hands."

Carrying His own wooden beam, Jesus was led away to a place called Golgotha (or Calvary), where Roman soldiers nailed Him to the cross. Then they lifted Him up for everyone to see. His first words from the cross were "Father, forgive them, for they do not know what they do" (Luke 23:34).

The Pain of the Cross (Mark 15:29–30, Luke 23:35–39)

Jesus' body felt terrible pain as He died on the cross. But He also suffered the shame of the crowd's insults. People walking by took something He'd said earlier and twisted it. They shouted, "Ah! You who are going to destroy the temple and rebuild it in three days, save Yourself and come down from the cross!" (Mark 15:29–30). Jewish religious leaders laughed at Him, saying, "He saved others; let Him save Himself" (Luke 23:35). Even the Roman soldiers (Luke 23:37) and one of the criminals at His side (Luke 23:39) mocked Him.

Jesus' Last Words

The Gospels contain seven statements that Jesus made while He hung on the cross:

- ▶ "Father, forgive them, for they do not know what they do" (Luke 23:34).

- ▶ To the repentant criminal hanging beside Him: "Truly I say to you, today you shall be with Me in paradise" (Luke 23:43).

- ▶ To His mother, Mary, and His disciple John: "Woman, behold, your son!" . . . "Behold, your mother!" (John 19:26–27).

- ▶ "My God, My God, why have You forsaken Me?" (Matthew 27:46, Mark 15:34).

- ▶ "I am thirsty" (John 19:28 NLV).

- ▶ "It is finished" (John 19:30).

- ▶ "Father, into Your hands I give My spirit" (Luke 23:46 NLV).

Jesus' Death (Matthew 27:45–56, Mark 15:33–39, Luke 23:46–56, John 19:28–30)

Around noon of the day Jesus was crucified, a strange darkness covered the land. Later, Jesus cried out to God the Father, "My God, My God, why have You forsaken Me?" (Matthew 27:46). When the time came for Jesus to die, He cried out, "It is finished" (John 19:30), and "Father, into Your hands I commend My spirit" (Luke 23:46). At the moment Jesus died, "the veil of the temple was torn in two from the top to the bottom" (Matthew 27:51). This miracle showed that a new way had been opened to God's presence.

The Burial of Jesus (Matthew 27:57–66, Mark 15:42–47, Luke 23:50–56, John 19:31–42)

After Jesus' death, Joseph of Arimathea—a Jewish religious leader but secret disciple of Jesus—asked Pontius Pilate for permission to bury the Lord's body. Pilate agreed. So Joseph took Jesus' body off the cross, placed Jesus in his own new tomb, and rolled a stone in front of it. Two women who had followed Jesus saw the burial. Then they went home to prepare more spices and perfumes for Jesus' body.

Joseph of Arimathea

Joseph was a wealthy member of the Sanhedrin—a Jewish group who held a lot of power. Because he was a secret disciple of Jesus, he took a big chance by standing against the Sanhedrin's decision to have Jesus executed (John 19:38). Joseph also helped with Jesus' burial.

Along with Nicodemus, Joseph wrapped the body in strips of linen mixed with good-smelling spices. Then Joseph placed Jesus in his own tomb, in a garden near the place of the crucifixion. This fulfilled an Old Testament prophecy: "He made His grave with the wicked and with the rich in His death because He had done no violence, nor was any deceit in His mouth" (Isaiah 53:9).

Jesus Rises from the Dead (Matthew 28:1–10, Mark 16:1–8, Luke 24:1–12, John 20:1–10)

In Matthew 20:18–19 (NLV), Jesus told His disciples, "Listen! We are going up to Jerusalem. The Son of Man will be handed over to the religious leaders and to the teachers of the Law. They will say that He must be put to death. They will hand Him over to the people who do not know God. They will make fun of Him and will beat Him. They will nail Him to a cross. Three days later He will be raised to life."

All those horrible things happened, exactly as Jesus said. But guess what? So did the good part about His resurrection!

The Empty Tomb (John 20:11–22)

Jesus, alive again, appeared first to a woman named Mary Magdalene. He had once cast seven demons out of her (Luke 8:2), and now she was one of His dearest friends. Mary had gone to Jesus' tomb very early on the Sunday morning after His death, and she wept outside. When she looked inside the tomb, Mary saw two angels in white, sitting where Jesus' body had been. When she turned away from the angels, she noticed a man standing nearby. It was Jesus, alive again! He then told her to go tell the other disciples what she had seen.

Why Does Jesus' Resurrection Matter?

The apostle Paul was not one of Jesus' original twelve disciples. But he became one of the most important leaders in the church in the years after Jesus. Paul wrote, "If Christ has not been raised, then our preaching is useless and your faith is also useless. . . . You are still in your sins" (1 Corinthians 15:14, 17).

Jesus' resurrection is proof of who He claimed to be. It shows that He can be trusted to keep His word in all things. If He had not kept the promise of His own resurrection, what reason would we have to follow Him? But because He lives, we know that He has defeated death—and those who follow Him will too.

The Risen Jesus Appears to Others (Numerous Passages)

Mary Magdalene was not the only person Jesus spent time with before returning to heaven. He visited a group of female followers (Matthew 28:9–10), His disciple Peter (Luke 24:34), and two men on the road to Emmaus (Luke 24:13–32). Jesus also saw all of the apostles except for Thomas (Luke 24:36–43, John 20:19–25), the apostles including Thomas (John 20:26–29), seven of His disciples on the shores of the Sea of Galilee (John 21:1–25), and all the disciples on a mountain in Galilee (Matthew 28:16–20, Mark 16:15–18). At other times, Jesus visited more than five hundred believers (1 Corinthians 15:6), His brother James (1 Corinthians 15:7), the apostles as He ate a meal with them (Acts 1:3–8, Luke 24:44–49), and His followers just before He rose up to heaven (Mark 16:19–20, Luke 24:50–53, Acts 1:9–12).

Jesus Restores Peter (John 21:15–25)

Peter was one of Jesus' closest friends. He was so devoted to Jesus that he once drew a sword to defend Him! But when Jesus was on trial for His life, Peter said he didn't even *know* Jesus—three times. After Jesus rose from the dead, though, He went out of His way to let Peter know that he was forgiven. Jesus told Peter what lay ahead for him—both in terms of his ministry and his own death.

The Great Commission

Matthew 28:16–20 and Mark 16:15–18 describe how Jesus prepared His disciples for their assignment after He returned to heaven. This was the Great Commission: "Go and make followers of all the nations. Baptize them in the name of the Father and of the Son and of the Holy Spirit. Teach them to do all the things I have told you. And I am with you always, even to the end of the world" (Matthew 28:19–20 NLV).

The disciples would end up changing the world for good. But first, they would need the power Jesus had promised.

MAIN ROAD

Christianity Begins (Acts)

The book of Acts—also called "Acts of the Apostles"—contains the history of the early church. A few weeks after Jesus returned to heaven, the early Christians were given God's gift of the Holy Spirit (Acts 2). This gave them the power to take the message of salvation to the world. The book of Acts also describes how a guy named Saul (later known as Paul) went from persecuting the church to becoming the greatest missionary in history.

Jesus Returns to Heaven (Acts 1)

After Jesus was raised from the dead, He stayed on earth for forty days. During that time, He proved to His disciples that He really was alive. And He gave them His final teaching about the kingdom of God. On the Mount of Olives, Jesus told them to stay in Jerusalem until God sent the Holy Spirit (Acts 1:4–5). Jesus promised them, "You will receive power when the Holy Spirit comes into your life. You will tell about Me. . .to the ends of the earth" (Acts 1:8 NLV). And then—after about thirty-three years on earth—Jesus returned to His Father in heaven.

The Ascension

Jesus' disciples stood amazed, watching Jesus ascend (rise up) back to heaven. Two angels in white appeared on the scene and said to them, "You men of the country of Galilee, why do you stand looking up into heaven? This same Jesus Who was taken from you into heaven will return in the same way you saw Him go up into heaven" (Acts 1:11 NLV).

The angels' message was clear: Jesus was coming back one day. . .but for now, the disciples had work to do! The book of Acts shows how they took this message to heart—and how the Holy Spirit helped them along the way.

Jesus' Promise of the Holy Spirit (Acts 1)

Acts 1:4–5 says that just before Jesus left for heaven, He told the disciples to stay in Jerusalem and wait for "the promise of the Father" to come. In case there was any question what that might be, Jesus explained: "For truly John baptized with water, but you shall be baptized with the Holy Spirit not many days from now." The disciples then returned to Jerusalem, where they gathered in "an upper room" (Acts 1:13). They and other believers prayed and waited.

The Church's Birthday (Acts 2)

God kept Jesus' promise on a Jewish holiday called Pentecost (Acts 2:1). Many Jews from around the world were in Jerusalem at the time. Suddenly, God sent the sound of rushing wind and "tongues of fire" that came to rest on each of Jesus' followers. These people began "speaking in tongues"—languages they didn't even know. But all visitors to the city knew what they were saying, in their own languages (verses 9–11)! The early Christians had all been filled with God's Holy Spirit. From then on, God would actually live inside believers!

SIDE ROAD

"Speaking in Tongues"

When the believers in Jerusalem were filled with the Holy Spirit, they began speaking in languages they didn't know. Visitors to Jerusalem—people from all over the world—could hardly believe their ears: "Now when this was reported outside, the multitude came together and were confounded, because every man heard them speak in his own language. And they were all amazed and marveled, saying to one another, 'Behold, are not all these who speak Galileans? And how do we hear every man in our own tongue, in which we were born? Parthians and Medes and Elamites and the dwellers in Mesopotamia, and in Judea, and Cappadocia, in Pontus and Asia, Phrygia and Pamphylia, in Egypt and in the parts of Libya around Cyrene, and visitors from Rome, Jews and proselytes, Cretans and Arabs—we hear them speaking in our tongues the wonderful works of God'" (Acts 2:6–11).

Peter Preaches Powerfully (Acts 2:14–47)

Many of those who saw the events of the day of Pentecost were amazed. But some made fun of what was happening. "These men are full of new wine," they said (Acts 2:13). But the apostle Peter—the same Peter who had just recently denied knowing Jesus—was now filled with the awesome power of the Holy Spirit. He courageously preached a sermon so powerful that about three thousand people came to faith in Jesus Christ (Acts 2:41)!

The Church Thrives (Acts 3–4)

The new church in Jerusalem grew very quickly. . .and the Jewish religious leaders were not happy. After Peter and John healed a lame man at the temple, Peter preached another powerful sermon, and thousands more came to faith in Jesus. The religious leaders arrested Peter and John and ordered them to stop preaching the name of Jesus. But Peter and John refused, saying, "If it is right to listen to you more than to God, you decide about that. For we must tell what we have seen and heard" (Acts 4:19–20 NLV). And so they did!

SIDE ROAD

The First Christian Martyr

It wasn't long before the religious leaders began persecuting—causing trouble for—the apostles and other believers. The first Christian to lose his life for his faith was a godly man named Stephen. When he told the Jewish leaders that they'd crucified God's Messiah, they became furious—so much so that they threw rocks at Stephen until he died (Acts 7:54–60). This made him Christianity's first "martyr."

Stephen's death kicked off terrible persecution against the church in Jerusalem. All the Christians except for the apostles ran away from the city. They scattered throughout Judea and Samaria and preached the gospel as they went.

The Church's Main Enemy (Acts 8:1–4)

Saul, later called Paul, was a Pharisee who was there where Stephen was killed. Saul hated Christians. He thought he was doing God's will when he had them imprisoned and killed (Acts 8:3; 22:4). He hated the very name of Jesus (Acts 26:9) and believed that His followers were blaspheming God. But that changed when Saul met Jesus in a very dramatic way.

Jesus Calls Saul to Serve Him (Acts 9:1–9)

One day, Saul was traveling to the city of Damascus, located in modern-day Syria. He wanted to arrest believers there and take them back to Jerusalem. Suddenly, a light from heaven surrounded him. Saul fell to the ground, blinded. A voice from heaven asked, "Saul, Saul, why are you persecuting Me?" (Acts 9:4). The voice identified Himself as Jesus. . .and then told Saul to go to the city and wait for His instructions (Acts 9:5–6). Still blind, Saul got up and continued to Damascus—but now for a totally different reason.

Peter's Odd Vision

God gave the apostle Peter a strange vision. He saw a sheet being let down from heaven by its four corners, filled with a bunch of animals that the Old Testament law said Jews shouldn't eat. In the vision, a voice from heaven told Peter, "Rise, Peter; kill and eat" (Acts 10:13), assuring him that God had made these animals clean (Acts 10:15). Peter didn't know what to make of it. But God used a Roman soldier named Cornelius to show him.

Since Cornelius was a Roman, Jews didn't want anything to do with him. But when God told Cornelius to meet with Peter, the Holy Spirit told Peter to accept Cornelius as a brother. Peter realized God was telling him that he should never think of anyone—even Gentiles—as "unclean" (Acts 10:28). After that, many Gentiles became Christians (see Acts 10).

Saul Meets a Christian Brother (Acts 9:10–17)

When Saul arrived in Damascus, the Christians there were nervous. They all knew the terrible things Saul had done to believers in and around Jerusalem. So when God told Ananias, a Christian in Damascus, to greet Saul, Ananias was confused. . .and a little bit frightened. But God told him, "Go! This man is the one I have chosen to carry My name among the people who are not Jews and to their kings and to Jews" (Acts 9:15 NLV).

Saul Begins Serving (Acts 9:18–35)

Ananias obeyed God's command. He greeted Saul, prayed for him, laid his hands on him, and told him what God had said. Saul received both his sight and the Holy Spirit (Acts 9:17). Then he was baptized (Acts 9:18). Saul began visiting the nearby synagogues (Jewish worship centers) and telling people about Jesus (Acts 9:20).

Saul later traveled and spent time in various places preparing for his life of service (Galatians 1:17–24). Then a respected Christian man named Barnabas asked him to help teach believers in the church at Antioch (Acts 11:25–26).

"Christians"

Today, a follower of Jesus Christ is called a "Christian." The book of Acts says, "The disciples were first called Christians in Antioch" (11:26). Antioch, about three hundred miles north of Jerusalem, was the center of the early Christian church. It was from Antioch that Paul launched the first of three missionary journeys.

Toward the end of his life, Paul stood trial for stirring up riots with his preaching. As Paul described his faith journey to Herod Agrippa II, the king said, "You almost persuade me to become a Christian" (Acts 26:28).

The word *Christian*, which means "follower of Christ," caught on. Followers of Jesus have been known as "Christians" ever since.

Paul's First Missionary Journey (Acts 13–14)

In Antioch of Syria, a group of godly "prophets and teachers" (Acts 13:1) were worshipping God and praying. The Holy Spirit spoke to them: "Separate Barnabas and Saul for Me for the work to which I have called them" (13:2). So Paul's first missionary journey began!

On this trip, he and Barnabas traveled to the seacoast city of Seleucia, the Mediterranean island of Cyprus, Pamphylia, the northern region of Galatia, *another* city called Antioch (in Pisidia), and finally back to Antioch of Syria. The whole trip took six to nine months.

Two More Journeys (Acts 15–21)

Paul's second journey is found in Acts 15–18, and the third in chapters 18–21. On his second trip, Paul's traveling companion was Silas. They preached and taught in many cities, staying in Corinth (in modern-day Greece) for about a year and a half. Much of the same happened on his third trip. This time, Paul stayed in Ephesus for over two years and later visited Corinth again. Finally, he returned to Jerusalem, where he was arrested and put in prison.

SIDE ROAD

The Jerusalem Council

At the end of their first missionary journey, Paul and Barnabas traveled to Jerusalem to meet with other Jewish believers. They wanted to talk about the many non-Jews who were joining the church. Should these people agree to become Jews before they became Christians? And what about the law of Moses? Was it necessary anymore?

After much prayer and discussion, the Jerusalem council issued four "rules" by which Gentile Christians should live: "That you abstain from meat offered to idols, and from blood, and from things that have been strangled, and from fornication. If you keep yourselves from these, you shall do well. Farewell" (Acts 15:29).

Paul's Missionary Legacy (Acts, the Letters of Paul)

Starting about AD 47, Paul traveled some ten thousand miles—many on foot—preaching the good news of salvation. He founded at least fourteen churches (perhaps as many as twenty). And he wrote many challenging, encouraging letters—including Romans, 1 and 2 Corinthians, Galatians, Ephesians, Philippians, and Colossians. Paul also mentored several people who continued his ministry after he was gone.

The End of Paul's Story (Acts 21–28)

Many people came to faith in Jesus when Paul preached. But some hated his message. Because he wouldn't stop talking about Jesus, Paul was threatened, beaten, and imprisoned. He ended his third missionary journey in Jerusalem, where he was arrested for preaching the name of Jesus. This arrest eventually led to his sailing for Rome—an adventurous trip that included a shipwreck and God's miraculous protection of all 276 people aboard.

The book of Acts ends with Paul living under house arrest in Rome. He was mostly free to do as he pleased, so he boldly preached and taught his visitors about Jesus. Though his biblical story ends with Paul in his own rented home (Acts 28:30), some church traditions say he was finally executed by Roman authorities.

What Are Epistles?

In scripture, the book of Acts is followed by twenty-one books that are actually letters (also called epistles). They were written to various churches or individuals. But these letters all have much to teach us today.

Paul wrote thirteen of these epistles: Romans, 1 and 2 Corinthians, Galatians, Ephesians, Philippians, Colossians, 1 and 2 Thessalonians, 1 and 2 Timothy, Titus, and Philemon.

The other New Testament letters are Hebrews (author unknown), James (probably by Jesus' half brother), 1 and 2 Peter (by the apostle Peter), 1, 2, and 3 John (by the apostle John), and Jude (by Jude, probably another half brother of Jesus).

The Bible ends with Revelation, which is the only New Testament book of prophecy.

7. THE END TIMES
Jesus' Return and the Renewal of All Things

MAIN ROAD

The Promise of Jesus' Return (Acts 1:10–11, Revelation)

As Jesus rose back up to heaven, two angels appeared to His disciples, saying that Jesus would return (Acts 1:11).

The Bible, in both the Old Testament and the New, has much to say about Jesus' return to earth and the end of time. All of these prophecies show that God has a clear plan in mind for rewarding His kids, punishing His enemies, and restoring all things.

Jesus' Return as Conquering King (Revelation 19)

Jesus came to earth the first time as the suffering Servant. But when He returns, it will be as conquering King:

> *Then I saw heaven opened. A white horse was standing there. The One Who was sitting on the horse is called Faithful and True. He is the One Who punishes in the right way. He makes war. His eyes are a flame of fire. He has many crowns on His head. His name is written on Him but He is the only One Who knows what it says. The coat He wears has been put in blood. His name is The Word of God. The armies in heaven were dressed in clean, white, fine linen. They were following Him on white horses. Out of His mouth comes a sharp sword to punish the nations. He will be the Leader over them using a piece of iron. He walks on the grapes where wine is made, pressing out the anger of God, the All-powerful One. On His coat and on His leg is the name written, "KING OF KINGS AND LORD OF LORDS."*

> REVELATION 19:11–16 NLV

Jesus Describes His Return

Over and over again, the Bible promises that Jesus will come back to this sad, broken world. He will defeat sin, provide justice, and make all things right. Shortly before His crucifixion, Jesus Himself told His disciples that He would return "in the clouds of the sky" to gather His people from all over the earth (Matthew 24:30–31 NLV). Another time, Jesus made this promise regarding His return: "And if I go and prepare a place for you, I will come again and receive you to Myself, that where I am, there you may be also" (John 14:3). What a beautiful promise to God's children!

Signs of the Times (Matthew 24–25, Mark 13, Luke 21)

Just before He was arrested and crucified, Jesus told His followers that nobody except His Father knows when He will return (Matthew 24:36).

Human beings can't say exactly when Jesus will come back. . .and we were never meant to. But we can read the "signs of the times" for hints that His return is near. In His "Olivet Discourse" (Matthew 24–25, Mark 13, and Luke 21), Jesus talked about nearly two dozen signs that His return is close. He encouraged Christians to watch and remain faithful.

The Rise of Antichrist (Revelation 13)

John wrote down a disturbing vision of two scary beasts and a dragon (Satan) in the end of time. Many believe the first beast stands for the way the nations of the world team up against God. . .and the second stands for the Antichrist. That is the evil person the apostle Paul called "[the] man of sin" and "the son of destruction" (2 Thessalonians 2:3). The Antichrist and his deeds are also described in Daniel 9:27 and 11:36–45.

666

Revelation 13:16–17 provides a frightening warning: the Beast "causes all, both small and great, rich and poor, free and bond, to receive a mark on their right hand or on their foreheads. . . that no man might buy or sell, except him who had the mark or the name of the beast, or the number of his name." This mark is often called "the mark of the Beast."

The next verse mysteriously identifies the "number" of the Beast as "six hundred and sixty-six." Nobody knows what the number 666 actually means. Throughout history, some have used the number to try to identify the Antichrist as Emperor Nero, various Catholic popes, and even some American presidents.

The Great Tribulation (Revelation 7)

Revelation 7:14 mentions a "great tribulation." This is the terrible time in which God will judge the world. The Bible says it will last seven years. Some Christians believe Jesus will take His followers to heaven before it starts, in an event called "the rapture." Others believe Christians will remain on earth for half of the tribulation. Still others believe Christians will stay on earth the whole seven years.

The tribulation begins when the Antichrist comes into power and makes an agreement with the nation of Israel (Daniel 9:27). The period will include wars, famines, plagues, and natural disasters as God punishes sinners everywhere on earth.

Armageddon (Revelation 16)

In Revelation 16:16, the term *Armageddon* refers to a huge future battle between God and the forces of evil. In the Hebrew language, the word means "Mount Megiddo." In this place, God will destroy the massive armies of the Antichrist before they can attack the city of Jerusalem. Here, Jesus will defeat the forces of evil once and for all (Revelation 19:15–16).

The Rapture

You won't find the word *rapture* in the Bible. It comes from a Latin word meaning "a carrying off" or "a snatching away." Many Christians believe that the rapture is a future event in which God takes His followers to heaven before He judges the earth. This idea comes from the apostle Paul in 1 Corinthians 15:51–52 (NLV): "We will not all die, but we will all be changed. In a very short time, no longer than it takes for the eye to close and open, the Christians who have died will be raised. It will happen when the last horn sounds. The dead will be raised never to die again. Then the rest of us who are alive will be changed."

And in his first letter to the Thessalonians, Paul said: "Those of us who are alive when the Lord comes again will not go ahead of those who have died. For the Lord Himself will come down from heaven with a loud call. The head angel will speak with a loud voice. God's horn will give its sounds. First, those who belong to Christ will come out of their graves to meet the Lord. Then, those of us who are still living here on earth will be gathered together with them in the clouds. We will meet the Lord in the sky and be with Him forever" (4:15–17 NLV).

Satan Is Defeated (Revelation 20)

The book of Revelation contains many scary images. There are terrible predictions of what will happen on earth in the end times. But Revelation ends with an encouraging message: God wins!

For thousands of years, Satan has worked hard to destroy people's hope. But Revelation describes Satan's future: "And the devil. . .was cast into the lake of fire and brimstone. . .and shall be tormented day and night forever and ever" (Revelation 20:10).

The Universe Is Restored (Revelation 21–22)

Jesus once said, "Heaven and earth shall pass away, but My words shall not pass away" (Mark 13:31). Revelation 21 explains that the old heaven and earth will be destroyed. . .and replaced by brand-new ones (verses 1–2)! When this all happens, "God shall wipe away all tears from their eyes, and there shall be no more death or sorrow or crying, nor shall there be any more pain, for the former things have passed away" (verse 4). From that moment on, the curse of sin will be gone forever (Revelation 22:3), and a perfect eternity will begin.

Go Deeper into God's Word!

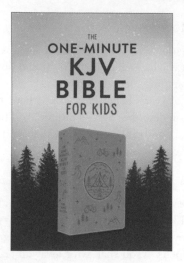

Kids can visualize what they read in the Bible through 80 full-color bonus pages explaining and illustrating key people, places, things, events, and ideas. Featuring the complete Old and New Testaments in the beloved, trusted King James Version, *The One-Minute KJV Bible for Kids* makes God's Word come to life for young readers.

Flexible DiCarta / 978-1-63609-522-6